# Close Encounters
## of the
## Furred Kind

Also by Tom Cox

*The Good, the Bad, and the Furry*

# Close Encounters
## of the
## Furred Kind

TOM COX

THOMAS DUNNE BOOKS
St. Martin's Press
New York

THOMAS DUNNE BOOKS.
An imprint of St. Martin's Press.

www.thomasdunnebooks.com
www.stmartins.com

The Library of Congress Cataloging-in-Publication Data is available upon request.

ISBN 978-1-250-07732-5 (hardcover)
ISBN 978-1-4668-8927-9 (e-book)

Our books may be purchased in bulk for promotional, educational, or business use. Please contact your local bookseller or the Macmillan Corporate and Premium Sales Department at 1-800-221-7945, extension 5442, or by e-mail at MacmillanSpecialMarkets@macmillan .com.

First published in Great Britain by Sphere, an imprint of Little, Brown Book Group, an Hachette UK company

First U.S. Edition: August 2016

10  9  8  7  6  5  4  3  2  1

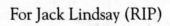

For Jack Lindsay (RIP)

# Close Encounters
## of the
## Furred Kind

# The Cat: a Folk Tale

Once upon a time, a man, a woman and a cat were walking through a deep forest. All three had walked for what felt like a thousand miles, and all but the smallest member of the party balanced precariously on blistered, swollen feet. Night had fallen only an hour before, but its polished granite blackness above the treetops seemed to hint at a stark permanence and corresponding adjustments to the way life would be lived. Just as the man and the woman felt that they could not possibly walk any more, they chanced upon a stone bothy at the edge of a small clearing. The bothy showed few signs of recent occupation: the man entered first and found only a strip of dirty, unspecified cloth, a broken tankard and the decayed skeleton of an apple core on its mud floor. Its roof had a hole, but this was covered by thick, twisted limbs of ivy, which for now would go some way to keeping out the advancing weather, which the woman could feel in her finger joints.

'Here?' she said.

'Here,' nodded the man.

They bedded down in the lone, draughty room beneath an old threadbare blanket given to her by her late mother, their tunics spread on top of it for extra warmth. An enchanted dancing spell of mist rose off the cold forest floor, covering the world in doubt. The cat, who had big deep eyes that seemed to hold innumerable secrets, began the evening sitting in the doorless doorway, listening to the nearby hoot of owls, then, having spied the tunics, nestled on top of those instead. By the time dawn arrived, the cat had somehow commandeered 85 per cent of the sleeping area while the man and woman, who were each roughly nine times the creature's size and largely furless, were squashed into the remaining 15 per cent, their limbs contorted in an awkward and painful fashion. Rising and inspecting the tunics, the man found welded to them a matted mixture of small leaves, hair and soil.

'You fucking wanker,' the man said to the cat. 'We only washed those last month.'

Later that morning, the man ventured out into the forest, killed two rabbits and filled a pail with water from a clear rushing river a mile away, surrounded by mossy boulders. The cat sat and watched with wry curiosity as the man and woman skinned, cooked and ate the rabbits. Then the man threw him the leftovers, which the cat gnawed on with something approaching enthusiasm. The woman poured the cat some of the clear river water into a bowl, which he refused, instead choosing to drink the rainwater from a rusty trough behind the building, which had all manner of unidentifiable old shit in it.

They could feel the dark teeth of midwinter gnashing at them now. Here was the final heavy push towards Solstice's new hope. The next day the man caught three more rabbits, roasted them on a bigger, angrier fire, and offered the cat a larger portion of the leftovers than before. The cat sniffed at this, then looked up into the man's eyes in a way that seemed to say, 'Nope, I've gone off this stuff already. Do you have anything else?'

Over the following weeks, the man and woman worked hard to transform the bothy into a home: the man walked to the river and caught fish, which the woman took to the town, some four miles away, on market day and traded for crockery, tools, milk, butter and soap. The man coppiced and whittled and hammered and chiselled and extended and improved. The days were long, partly because there was endless work to do, but also because the cat insisted on waking the man and woman up before daybreak by meowing at the top of his voice and knocking stuff off the new shelves the man had built. The three of them sat by the fire at night: the woman working on a poem by the flickering light, the man so tired he could only stare blankly into the flames, and the cat cleaning himself in an officious manner that suggested he was getting ready for an important yet clandestine cat ceremony in the near future. Sometimes, while the woman tried to write her poetry, the cat would get on her lap and stick his bottom in her face, obscuring her view and smudging her fine calligraphy with his paws. Later, he would continue to dominate the bed, leaving more small leaves, hair and soil on the new blankets that had replaced the tunics as bedding. He'd also occasionally pop off into the forest to kill mice, which he would bring back and leave half eaten on the bothy's floor. The cat was generally very unpredictable when it came to food. Some days he preferred rabbits caught in the part of the forest to the east of the bothy, and some days he preferred rabbits caught in the part of the forest to the west of the bothy, but the man and woman were buggered if they knew why.

One morning a visitor came to call, a tall gentleman with an angular face and the tiny eyes of an untrustworthy bird. He said he worked for the squire of the local parish, and he had a proposal: if the man and the woman would concede ownership of the bothy to the squire, who deemed it a perfect hunting lodge, he would reward them with more money than they had seen in their lives.

'Take three sunsets to think it over if you like,' said the tall gentleman, jingling some coins in a leather purse. 'By the way, did you know you had a mouse's spleen stuck to your big toe?'

That night by the fire the man and woman faced a tough decision: they had worked hard on their new dwelling and were looking forward to starting a family there, but with the squire's money, they would be able to set up home almost anywhere they chose. By the glow of the fire, they examined their hands, which, due to a life of constant toil, were as gnarled and wrinkled as those of men and women twice their age born of more noble stock. As they did so, they knew which choice they would make.

The night before the man and the woman were due to vacate the bothy, a party was thrown there, a celebration as lavish as any small makeshift dwelling in the woods had ever known. In a gesture of goodwill, the squire provided limitless ale, eclectic soups and a freshly slaughtered wild hog. Better still, this was not just any wild hog: this was Big John, the grandest and haughtiest hog of the forest, whom every hunter for miles around had been trying to bring down for as long as memory would allow, and whom the squire had finally slain earlier that day. A minstrel played songs celebrating the deeds of the afternoon, and the bawdy ones of outlaws of centuries past in the Green Wood, and a few of the squire's men danced with the woman – though not, the man was fairly sure, in a dodgy way which involved trying to cop a sneaky feel. The cat ate like a feline king, then bedded down on the large comfortable stomach of one of the night's early casualties: Edgar, the fattest of all the squire's men. Edgar was now paralytic and emitting stale odours from at least two of his orifices, but the cat was largely relaxed about odours, unless they were soapy or astringent, and Edgar did possess an unusually soft tunic. Before this, the cat had spent a good hour or so batting a button that had come loose from another of the men's tunics around the floor. The woman saw this, and it kind of pissed her off, as she'd spent a lot of the previous week making a cloth mouse for the cat, which he'd indifferently inspected once then totally ignored.

It had been a grand night, but the next morning, when the man and woman woke up, a discomfort and self-hatred set in, compounded by their hangovers. How easily they'd given away what they'd worked lovingly to make theirs, in exchange for monetary gain. The squire and his men were still asleep, yet somehow the man and woman already felt unwelcome in their home of many months, so they gathered their possessions and quietly set off into the cool spring morning. The cat followed a few paces to their rear, and they thought about what a good cat he was, how beautiful and plush his fur was and how lucky they were that he followed them from place to place like this. When all was said and done, at least they still had his love. The cat, for his part, was sort of torn, if he was being totally honest, since he could still smell the remains of the wild hog and remember how soft that tunic was. But, he concluded, the bothy would not be permanently occupied with feeders, now it belonged to the squire, who would be using it as more of a weekend place, and the man and woman were OK sorts, especially when you considered how many cat-hating scumbags there were out there.

In time, the man and the woman found a new house, made it their own and raised a family in it. The money wasn't quite as much as it had seemed at first and soon ran out, but they found other ways to get by. They didn't quite live happily ever after, since people never actually do. It would be more accurate to say that existence was made more enjoyable than not by an ample sprinkling of fleeting, epiphanic moments of happiness, which were rendered more meaningful by being set against a more customary backdrop of mundanity and grey struggle.

Fortunately, they lived with a cat, and living with a cat has a way of helping prepare people for life's peaks and troughs.

The cat lived to a ripe old age. But that was no big deal for him. He'd lived numerous times previously, and had seen some dark shit you could not even dream of.

# Winter is Coming

It was early autumn in 2013, and I was sitting on the floor in my living room in Norfolk, talking on the telephone to my mum, who was at her house in Nottinghamshire. Around me, as far as I could see, were cardboard boxes. On top of one of the boxes nearest to me was my very large, very hairy cat, Ralph.

'I think you might regret this,' said my mum.

'It will be OK,' I said. 'There's not *that* much stuff, and it will save me a load of money.'

'You're surely not thinking of doing it completely on your own?'

'No. Seventies Pat is going to drive over and help, at least for most of the journeys. He used to work for removal firms. He's pretty strong.'

'Raaaalpppph!'

'And the two of you are doing this in a van? What kind of van? I think you're severely underestimating. Two people is nothing, even if Seventies Pat's a big bloke.

You've probably got a lot more stuff to take than you think, and it's going to be very stressful.'

'Raaaalpppph!'

'Say that again?'

'I didn't say anything. That was just Ralph, Ralphing.'

'Oh, right.'

'Raaaalpppph! RaaraaaraaalllPH!'

'So how *is* Ralph at the moment?'

'He's OK. A bit anxious. He came in with a slug on his back earlier.'

'Again? How many's that this month?'

'Twelve, I think. That I know of, anyway. There could have been others.'

'Raaaaaallllllllllllllllllph!'

It was a frequent habit of Ralph's to join in with telephone calls from my landline – particularly those which, like this one, involved a somewhat fraught topic. His input largely consisted of either meowing his own name or sitting on the receiver at a point when he felt the conversation had run its natural course. He had always been a loud, opinionated cat, but he had been particularly vocal and agitated over the last few weeks, as the boxes had begun to pile up around him and a couple of his favourite scratching posts – items that, in their younger, more healthy days, I'd still had the audacity to call 'chairs' – had vanished to the charity shop.

Ralph had a kind of mutton-chopped, early 1970s rock star look about him that, despite his advancing age and popularity with molluscs, retained a certain twinkle. If he'd been a person, he would have been the kind you often found wearing a velvet jacket and a cravat. People frequently thought he was a Norwegian forest cat, or some other fancy longhair breed from the baffling, pampered world of pedigrees, but these assumptions were incorrect: Ralph's mum had been a common or garden tabby from Romford and his dad an all-black bruiser who would, in the words of his owners, 'bang anything on four legs'. I suppose at a push you might have called Ralph a Thetford Forest cat, but that was about it. Whatever the case, he was the most visually appealing of my cats, and seemed very aware of this fact. In keeping with his rock star image, he was known to have the odd celebrity tantrum, swanning around the house, climbing furniture and kicking vases and houseplants to the floor, all the while maintaining a steady stream of self-aggrandising

dialogue. Recently, the frequency and pitch of these tantrums had increased to the point that, only yesterday, while meow-shouting 'RAaaaallllph', he'd taken a running jump onto my sideboard, slid along the surface using the sleeve of a rare 1970s folk record as a skateboard, then, depositing the sleeve and those of two other similarly cherished records on the floor, run across the room and pulled a spider plant off a windowsill.

Ralph's unease was understandable. In just over a week, if all went to plan, he would be moving from a house that, for almost a decade, had functioned as his own little version of Cat Paradise; a Cat Paradise in which, to his own mind, he was a kind of sideburned Hippie King. In a sense, this was Ralph's world, and the rest of us – me, my girlfriend Gemma and our three other cats, The Bear, Roscoe and Ralph's sinewy, foul-mouthed brother Shipley – just lived in it. He swaggered around these large, airy rooms, soaking up their ample sunlight, his only real niggles in life a metal clothes horse he was unaccountably terrified of and an occasional need to bat Shipley into line with a big white fluffy paw. Outside, he had a habitat – green, fertile, leafy, abutted by a lake – which he had come to rely upon equally as his playground, his nightclub and his open-all-hours rodent buffet.

Sure, there had been foes and nemeses for Ralph, but all of these had drifted away. Pablo, defeated ginger opponent in The Great Four Year Cat Flap War of the previous decade, had long since gone to live with my ex. A succession of feral interlopers had been vanquished.

After a few tussles, even Alan, the ex-stray who now lodged with my next-door neighbours Deborah and David, seemed to have finally ceded to Ralph's dominance. Mike, our latest feral – a cat Gemma and I had initially referred to simply as 'The Wino' – had clearly long ago been defeated by life, and posed no real threat. Nope: this was Ralph's place, and he'd never felt more at home here. So why on earth would I want to take him away from it?

This was a question I'd asked myself several times over the last few weeks. The big overriding answer was money. In short, I'd run out of it. I had limped on for a few years, trying to convince myself otherwise, but I could no longer afford to stay in a high-maintenance house with a mortgage this big. Gemma, who was from Devon, increasingly missed home and, not having found work in Norfolk, had taken a temporary job back in the West Country, which meant that she was away for more than half of each month. After a decade here, I also fancied a change: a new environment, possibly even a completely different environment, far away. But the further I'd got into a three-month DIY marathon in an attempt to present it in its most favourable state, the more I fell in love with my weird, topsy-turvy, mid-twentieth-century house all over again.

Sure, the building whose previous owners had named it the Upside Down House had been an absolute bastard to heat, and bore more than a passing resemblance to a 1960s doctor's surgery, but it had been a happy house, so often full of light and people. And, yes, OK, there had been that time last year when my neighbour David had woken up to find a tent pitched at the bottom of his garden and discovered a paralytic stranger in it with a gun aimed at the adjacent lake, but we were living in a dangerous modern world and you had to be realistic. You might find a good home, but really, were you ever going to be too far away from a drunken man in a tent in a nearby garden, having a nervous breakdown and trying to shoot ducks with an air rifle? In the economic climate of 2013 I was lucky to own a house at all, not to mention a very nice one in a lovely county such as Norfolk. Now, as Ralph climbed up the fitted bookshelves near the telephone, hung off them and meowed 'Raaalph!', I felt a fair bit of empathy for him: part of me wanted to cling to the same shelves with my claws and meow 'Raaalph!', too.

My mum always watched me with great concern when it came to matters surrounding house moves. When I was growing up, she and my dad moved a lot, taking a few regrettable turns in the process, and she'd always been keen to pass on her wisdom and make sure I didn't make the same mistakes, or new ones of my own. Such as, say, trying to move the contents of a large three-bedroom home and overstuffed loft alone, in order to save myself a few hundred quid, because my bank account was in the red.

With this in mind, I changed the subject. 'Where's Dad? In the garden?'

'I'M HERE,' said my dad, who had a habit of listening in on the other line during telephone conversations, and, much like Ralph, adding his own high-volume non sequiturs to the mix.

'Ooh,' said my mum, startled. 'Where did you come from?'

'ME MUM'S WOMB. IN NOTTINGHAM. IN 1949,' said my dad.

'What have you been up to today?' I asked him.

'ME AND FLOYD HAVE BEEN HUNTING TOGETHER. WE WENT OUT IN THE FIELD AT THE BACK. HE'S STILL OUT THERE NOW. I THINK HE'S GOT THE SCENT OF A VOLE. YOU CAN SEE IT IN HIS EYES: HE'S GOT THE RED MIST.'

Floyd was my mum and dad's cat: a one year-old, Rorschach-faced, black and white whirlwind who had recently made a smooth transition from impossibly cute, wool-chasing kittenhood to serial-killing adolescence. After a few catless years, my dad, who had never previously been the most devout cat person, had found an unlikely companion in Floyd. The two of them – sometimes joined by Floyd's pal from next door, a ghostly white cat named Casper – did pretty much everything together. When my dad climbed a ladder to clean the windows or prune a clematis, Floyd climbed it with him. When my dad took his midday nap on the bed, or in the shady part of the garden he called Compost Corner, Floyd could invariably be found asleep alongside him.

If my dad arrived in his workroom to find Floyd resting at his desk on his chair, he declined to disturb him and instead kneeled beside him, or pulled up an uncomfortable wooden stool from the opposite side of the room. When I'd last been up to Nottinghamshire to visit them,

and my dad had emerged from the car wielding several shopping bags, it came as a slight surprise that Floyd wasn't following behind him, carrying a bag of flavoured deli counter sausages between his teeth. 'Hunting together', which took place in the field to the rear of their house, was a new activity for Floyd and my dad, who had recently celebrated his sixty-fourth birthday. I wasn't sure precisely what it involved, but I knew it wasn't actual hunting on my dad's part, but that it did fill a certain chasm in his life that had been there for around thirty years, since I'd last played games of Army with him.

'I'VE LEFT HIM TO CARRY ON ON HIS OWN AS I HAD SOME LOGS THAT NEEDED CHOPPING,' my dad continued.

'So why are you here now, interrupting us and not chopping the logs?' asked my mum, reasonably.

'TOM,' continued my dad, ignoring the question. 'LISTEN. THIS IS IMPORTANT. DID I TELL YOU ABOUT FLOYD AND THE SHEEP NEXT DOOR? I DON'T THINK I DID, DID I? THEY'VE PUT SOME SHEEP IN THE GARDEN TO KEEP THE GRASS SHORT. I WENT OVER THERE YESTERDAY TO GET SOME CORN ON THE COB I GREW IN ROGER AND BEA'S VEG PATCH, AND FLOYD AND CASPER FOLLOWED ME. I DON'T THINK FLOYD OR CASPER HAVE EVER SEEN SHEEP BEFORE, AND YOU COULD SEE THEM BOTH GOING "FOOKIN' 'ELL", AS THEY CAME AROUND THE CORNER. ONE OF THE RAMS, A REAL BIG HARD-LOOKING BASTARD, A JACOB'S SHEEP, STARTED COMING TOWARDS THEM, MEANING BUSINESS. FLOYD WOULD HAVE HAD HIM IF I HADN'T TOLD HIM NOT TO. THERE WERE SOME PEOPLE CAMPING OVER THERE YESTERDAY, TOO. I CAUGHT ONE OF THEM IN OUR GREENHOUSE, TOP-DRESSING A MARROW.'

'Anyway, Mick,' said my mum. 'We were talking about next week. Tom's decided not to hire a removal company and to do it all himself. I think he's mad.'

'ALL SOLICITORS ARE BASTARDS. MOST STRESSFUL THING IN THE WORLD, MOVING HOUSE,' said my dad. 'EVEN MORE STRESSFUL THAN GETTING DIVORCED OR DYING.'

'But you've never died or got divorced, so how do you know?' I said.

'I JUST DO. I'M SIXTY-FOUR AND I'VE BEEN UP SINCE FIVE O'CLOCK.'

'I've actually been up since five today as well,' I replied, but the last two words were lost, due to Ralph sitting on the receiver.

'Raalllllllppppppppph,' said Ralph.

'Can you stop doing that, please?' I asked Ralph. 'It's really rude.'

'Raaaaallllo!' said Ralph.

Part of me knew my dad was right: having very nearly died in hospital as a four-year-old and got divorced three decades later, I couldn't quite convince myself that either event was as stressful as the ten occasions on which I'd moved house as an adult. I'd naively hoped it would be simpler this time. One of the most stressful factors around selling a house and buying another is timing: the agonising possibility of finding your dream place, only to lose it when your own sale falls through. I was in no financial position to purchase another house, so by default had the luxury of exempting myself from that particular kind of conveyancing angst. Yet the longer the process of this move went on, the less of a luxury it seemed. The more obsessively I surfed property websites for rented accommodation, the more I realised that I wanted to find a rented house just like my own, the more

I realised such a house did not currently exist. I even began to backdate my searches on the property websites that kept old listings up, just to convince myself that at some point in the last couple of years, somewhere there had been an affordable, feline-friendly house to rent in rural or semi-rural surroundings that had fitted book-shelves and looked like the annexe of a 1960s doctor's surgery.

Like a lot of cat owners, I tended to ask two questions of any potential new home. The first was, 'Will the cats be happy here?' The second was, 'Do I like it?' If the answer was 'yes' to both, and Gemma liked the place too, I could begin to ask more practical questions. This instantly ruled out a vast number of houses in my price range. If I was honest, despite my misgivings about selling my house, I had a feeling in my bones that a move was right for me and Gemma; my real worry was about how the cats would deal with it. None more so than The Bear, an elderly owl poet who had, seemingly to his own immense confusion, ended up in a feline body.

The Bear was eighteen now, could no longer retract his claws, walked with a somewhat camp arthritic wobble and divided much of his time between the house's bal-cony and an old cardboard box, on which I'd scribbled the phrase 'Hotel Catifornia' in black marker pen. When The Bear emerged from his balcony or from Hotel Catifornia ('You can check out any time you like, but you can never leave . . .') it was invariably to follow me from room to room, staring at me with his big green eyes in a manner which seemed to ask the pivotal question:

'Can you tell me why I am a cat, please?' If The Bear was a human, he'd probably have been the kind who listened to records by The Smiths and Leonard Cohen. Opinion was divided on what was truly going on in his mind. Gemma and I believed he was an intellectual empath, who spent his days agonising over the world's countless problems. My parents, by contrast, thought he was senile. 'THAT CAT'S LOST IT,' my dad announced during their last visit. 'THE LIGHTS ARE ON BUT THERE'S NOBODY HOME.'

The Bear, who'd originally been not only my ex's cat, but my ex's ex's cat, had been a wilful, troubled cat in his youth. Old age, though, appeared to suit him. It seemed, in a Morgan Freeman sort of way, to be the time when he'd discovered the True Him. I actually found it quite hard to picture The Bear in his early and middle years now, so charismatic was his more wizened, philosophical incarnation. The eighteen-year-old Bear was polite, gentle, quizzical and companionable. My conviction that he was a right-thinking feline philosopher somehow seemed reinforced by the fact that he remained the only cat I had ever met who liked broccoli. Not for The Bear the rodent slaughter and territorial squabbles of his contemporaries. He was above that kind of thing, an animal of far greater nuance.

All four cats hassled for food in different ways: Ralph shouted 'Raaallllph!', Shipley usually called me a shit satchel in cat language and used my leg as a climbing frame, while perhaps most strangely of all, Roscoe, our lone female cat, preferred to dance across the floor on her hind legs, as if slapping paws with strangers in an imaginary disco bowling alley. The Bear's approach was more subtle. He'd simply look deep into my eyes, let out a tiny 'meeeoop', then nod towards the cupboard where I kept the cat food.

As a rule, the cats were no longer allowed on our bed, due to Gemma's asthma, but The Bear was so ineffably sweet we couldn't help making an exception every so often for him. 'Really? For *me*?' his eyes seemed to say, as he settled apprehensively on the duvet in a series of meticulous, circular padding manoeuvres. 'I'm just so . . . honoured. I really don't know what to say.' The Bear's spine felt more brittle than it once had and he moved more awkwardly, but his fur shone, and in the last couple of years he'd required the services of our local vet barely half as much as any of the other cats. He had been for a rare visit not all that long ago, after which, due to his unusually large appetite and slight weight loss of late, he'd been tested for an overactive thyroid gland, but the tests had come back negative. A few months on, he was plumper and glossier than ever. I knew The Bear couldn't live for ever, but another part of me was starting to wonder if the old, stagnant rain he slurped from his favourite watering can on the balcony every day was in fact an elixir of eternal life, its formula mixed

clandestinely under a full moon while the rest of the house slept.

I'd long maintained that The Bear's hypersensitive ears could detect the sound of conveyancing at a hundred paces, but this time he seemed wise to the move from the moment the estate agent stepped through the door, tape measure in hand.

'I'm afraid we can't have any pets in the pictures,' said the agent's photographer, spotting The Bear on the bed, as he took the photos of my exhaustively spruced and decluttered rooms. This I did not understand at all: I'd always been *more* attracted to a house when I glimpsed the reflection of an errant cat in a mirror, curled up on a bed or standing defiantly on a kitchen work surface in a photo on the Rightmove or Zoopla websites.'But you can't take photos of the house without The Bear!' I wanted to protest. 'The Bear *is* this house.' However, because I'm painfully English and polite, I didn't, and instead meekly and obediently moved The Bear to the balcony, his deep, betrayed eyes burning into me all the while.

'Sorry,' the photographer continued. 'I don't mind being near them but I can't touch them.' I couldn't quite work out what he meant by 'them': cats in general, or specifically elderly academic frustrated diplomat cats whose eyes drilled into your soul.

Far more than Ralph's increased Ralphing, Shipley's shouts of 'Spunk box!' and 'Piss officer!' and a new, vaguely perceptible nervousness in Roscoe's manner, it was those questioning looks from The Bear that made me feel I was a terrible person for moving house. 'So you're really doing this?' The Bear seemed to be saying to me. 'After all we've been through together to get here?' The Bear's longevity might have been put down to many factors – an innate sense of his own limitations that many other cats lacked; his quiet literary lifestyle; a diet containing just the right mix of rainwater, mechanically recovered meat and broccoli – but I knew that a big part of it was almost certainly due to his happiness and stability here, in this house, for the last decade. If I was going to move The Bear again, it would have to be to a place where he, and the other cats, would be at least as comfortable and happy as they'd been here: a place where there were no major worries about roads, with a bit of green outdoor space and enough indoor space to give all four cats as much chance as possible to peacefully coexist. An extra plus for The Bear, whose joints were getting stiffer all the time, would be a staircase that wasn't formidably steep.

All of this considerably narrowed the available pool of rental properties. Then there was the fact that landlords seemed to have tightened up their rules on pets in the eleven years since I'd last signed a tenancy contract. Many times while house-hunting, I would tell a letting agent 'I have cats', yet somehow what it would always feel like I was saying was, 'I have a large, volatile dragon who likes to party.' Around half of the population of the UK lives with one or more cats, but, as a prospective renter, being in the majority suddenly reduced me to the status of an untrustworthy leper. 'But one of them isn't really like a cat at all,' I wanted to protest to the agents I spoke to.

'He's more like a small version of David Attenborough with fur.' At least I'd been lucky enough to find some buyers for my house instantly: an impossibly elderly couple who were more or less the exact opposite of the buyers I'd imagined, and who stalked slowly yet purposefully around the place making a gradual, slightly surreal inspection of my possessions – a log cabin quilt made by my mum and a woodcut of a fox, for example – and asking if they would be included in the sale. After a few days they decided to withdraw their offer, having come to their senses and realised that, what with each recently passing their hundred and seventy-fourth birthdays, a three-storey building with East Anglia's steepest garden might not be a practical option. My replacement buyers – who, again luckily, followed immediately – were far less incongruous: two friendly civil servants wanting to escape the Home Counties commuter sprawl, who would be bringing with them a grumpy old ginger cat called Doris and a passion for mid-twentieth-century interior design. But they needed to move quickly. Which was fine by me, and entirely feasible if you overlooked the fact that Gemma and I were yet to come even close to deciding which part of the country we wanted to move to, let alone which house.

Our initial search had taken place in Gemma's home county of Devon, a place whose clear rushing rivers, wild moors, craggy prehistoric woodland and jagged, vertiginous coastline had been having an increasingly seductive effect on me for over a decade. House-hunting from 360 miles away was not easy. Out of absolute necessity I'd

sold my car a few months before to fund the improvements to my house, so visits to the fairly remote bits of
Devon we were searching in required me to use a hire
vehicle. Usually, by the time I had picked this up, found
a viewing time convenient for everyone concerned and
made the cross-country trip, the best houses we were
looking at had been snapped up. All of the few places left
to view that allowed pets fell short in at least one way:
they were too expensive, unsafe for cats, too remote for
Gemma, who was a non-driver, or had dingy rooms that
smelt like feet. In the midst of all this, I made calls to our
solicitor, whose indolence was putting me in severe jeopardy of losing the sale. Climbing tussocky hillocks and
walls in a desperate bid to get phone reception, I'd finally
get through to him, then invariably be cut off at the conversation's most vital juncture. Why had he not made a
call to the building regulations department like he'd
promised to, leaving my buyers convinced they'd lost the
house? Why was he sitting on forms I'd filled in weeks
ago, as if incubating them like some overweight chicken
in a posh shirt? At the end of my tether, I opted to take
the bits of conveyancing he couldn't be bothered to do
into my own hands and found them surprisingly simple.
But still the big question remained: where would we live?

Much as Gemma and I loved Devon, the idea of
moving there terrified us. Actually, that's not true. The
idea of moving there made Gemma feel warm inside and
me feel inspired, nervous and excited. The idea of moving
four cats there terrified us. This would entail a journey in
which we kept The Bear, Ralph, Shipley and Roscoe in

carriers in a car for around six hours, and that was only if we were lucky and didn't run into any big traffic jams. Rethinking, we began to widen our criteria to include much of the area between Devon and Norfolk, reasoning towards a more moderate first step west. We also continued to search in Norfolk itself, since neither of us had completely abandoned the idea of continuing to live there. But so much choice, far from being freeing, had a dizzying, tyrannical effect, sending me off on irrational bug-eyed, last-minute drives to unknown territory, and frantic local research missions that left me feeling like a five-year-old who'd been spun around repeatedly by his arms in a big confusing garden. 'I have seen a nice, almost affordable house near the village of Tubney Wood, one hundred and seventy miles away, and I cannot call the letting agent because it is Sunday and they are closed, and I have no knowledge of Tubney Wood, or what it's fundamentally about as a place, but I still have a few hours until the hire car is due back at the depot,' I would reason to myself. 'I know! I will drive to Tubney Wood, to check out the house from the outside, and confirm whether its garden wall really is too high for cats to climb and reach the adjacent road, as the picture on the letting agent's website suggests.'

After two heartbreaking near-misses on cat-friendly places – the first a quiet, church-owned town house necessitating the submission of a lengthy 'tenant's essay', whose junior estate agent incorrectly assured us 'Don't worry! You'll get it!', the second a one-storey, two-bed modernist architectural masterpiece whose rent had been capped at a strangely affordable price due to its lovely bearded architect landlord's wish for artists to live there, and which I was three agonising hours too late in applying for – I arrived back in Norfolk from yet another cross-country drive, blurry-pupilled, muddle-brained and spent, with nine days to go until the completion date on the sale, and proceeded to fill the tank of my diesel hire car with petrol. As I sat on the grass verge, half a mile farther up the road, and awaited the tow truck, I called to cancel the borderline insane viewing I'd arranged in an uncharted part of Somerset the following day and decided to admit defeat. I'd not only been trying too hard, not wanting to let anyone down – Gemma, The Bear, Ralph, Roscoe or Shipley – but also hoping to find a writing haven I could fall in love with which would comprehensively replace my existing house in my affections. I would opt for a different approach: I would, quite simply, find us somewhere to live.

Back in early summer, when we hadn't officially been looking for a house in or near Norwich, the place was full of attractive, light, cat-friendly places to rent on quiet roads. Now, four months later, the one feline-accommodating place that fitted our budget, timescale and most basic requirements was a fairly nondescript bungalow on the edge of the city with a garden made almost solely of concrete. Even securing a viewing for this required a certain amount of subterfuge. Shattered from my many drives west, the diesel incident and sleep-less nights worrying about conveyancing, I'd visited the letting agent in person, looking, if not in the midst of homelessness, then as if I was doing a pretty convincing dress rehearsal for it. It hadn't occurred to me that being tired, sorely in need of a haircut and wearing old clothes would disqualify you for eligibility for a small, one-storey 1970s house near Norwich, but I'd barely stepped in the door and it was clear that the lady at the front desk wasn't getting a great vibe from my ancient charity shop duffle coat.

'Nope, sorry,' she told me snippily when I asked about whether the bungalow's landlord would take cat-owning tenants. 'Absolutely no pets on that one.'

'Oh, that's a shame,' I said. 'Do you have anything else of a similar kind?'

'No, nothing at the moment,' she said. 'Sorry.'

At which point, to make it doubly clear that it was time for me to leave, she swivelled her chair rather the-atrically back towards her computer monitor and the more pressing tasks of the day which, from what I could gather from the travel agent's homepage open in her browser window, involved an imminent holiday to the San Lucianu beach resort in Corsica.

Undeterred, on arriving home I called the lettings agency again, putting on the respectable voice of some-one who owned a far nicer coat and explaining that I was a writer who owned cats and would like to view the bungalow. The agent's voice sounded very similar to that of the one I'd spoken to earlier in the day, but I couldn't be sure if it was her. Whatever the case, within a few minutes I'd established that the landlord was very happy to accept cat-owning tenants and arranged a viewing for the next day.

'ALL ESTATE AGENTS ARE BASTARDS,' said my dad when I told him about this episode. 'I CAN SEE WHERE THEY WERE COMING FROM WHEN IT CAME TO THAT COAT, THOUGH. NEXT TIME YOU'RE ON A COUNTRY WALK, YOU SHOULD TAKE IT OFF AND LEAVE IT AT THE SIDE OF THE ROAD. THE RSPCA WILL COME AND TAKE IT AWAY. COME TO THINK OF IT, ARE YOU SURE THE LETTINGS AGENCY DIDN'T MISHEAR YOU AND THINK YOU ASKED IF THE LANDLORD ACCEPTED COATS?'

The bungalow was hardly ideal, but idealism was out of the question at this stage. The garden resembled the kind of small down-at-heel car park you might find at the rear of a suburban dry-cleaner; the toilet floor was straight from a neglected 1980s shopping arcade and the council tax was extortionate, presumably due to the fact that from the kitchen window you could just glimpse some of the rooftops of houses owned by rich people. On the other hand, it was warm, clean, within walking distance of several of our friends and three or four of our favourite pubs, positioned at the end of a quiet cul-de-sac and had an area of rough ground to the side of it that promised to be a prime feline roaming area. I began to think of the place primarily as a retirement bungalow for The Bear: a cosy new hideaway for him, complete with single-storey layout and, courtesy of Gemma and me, round-the-clock catering.

It had to be noted, though, that The Bear's three furry housemates showed little inclination towards retirement. Ralph and Shipley were a little lazier than they'd once been, certainly, but between them still kept up a weekly vole and mouse count of around one per day. These rodents would very rarely get completely devoured, being instead either abandoned completely intact or with just their faces or rear ends remaining. In the former scenario, I'd often arrive in the kitchen to find The Bear – who'd never, to my knowledge, killed anything – standing over the corpse looking despairing and mournful, as if steeling himself for the thankless task of informing its next of kin. Twelve years of living with Ralph and Shipley and dodging vole faces and mouse innards had made me nimble on my feet, and I was hardened to the clean-up process, but rapidly diminishing floor space and clutter in the build-up to the move made matters more treacherous. So far during packing, I'd found a decomposing mouse in an old Scrabble box and a shrew's face folded into one of the dust sheets I'd been using while decorating. I sensed I'd only scratched the surface here, and that the unpacking process was going to be full of new and terrible discoveries.

Roscoe, too, was busy, but in a less bloodthirsty way. She was a small, cartoonish-looking cat, with shocked button eyes. At the tip of her black tail was a tiny, endearing smudge of white – a distinguishing feature that Shipley had briefly shared on the day I'd painted our stair

rail in gloss magnolia. Despite Roscoe's somewhat vacant looks, she maintained the industrious air of a cat who was constantly running late for an important corporate PowerPoint presentation. Even those somewhat over-dramatic arrivals of hers at feeding time, on her hind legs with her paws in the air, gave off the suggestion that she was squeezing us into a tight schedule: that we should be grateful for her presence, and perhaps offer her a high five or two by way of thanks. Of all the cats, Roscoe was the one I was least worried about transferring to a new house. She'd not had as long as the other cats to get truly established in this environment – Gemma and I had adopted her only a year and a half earlier, when she'd been just a few months old – and, despite being physically

vulnerable, a permakitten in size, she possessed an independence the three others didn't. You wouldn't find her
meowing her own name, swearing petulantly in your face
for no reason or staring up from the kitchen floor, con-
templating the void of existence. She was, all told, a bit
aloof, but in the feline dynamic of the house, having one
aloof cat was actually OK: it served to counterbalance
the other three somewhat needy ones. Before Roscoe's
arrival, Shipley had repeatedly bullied The Bear, shouting
monstrous insults in his face and interrupting his meditation sessions by clocking him on the head, but this had
calmed down noticeably, largely as a result of Roscoe
comprehensively decking Shipley whenever he got out of
hand. On these occasions Shipley's face would express
the same shock and fear a football hooligan's might after
being kicked powerfully in the testicles by a small female
child.

Roscoe had grown into her name: she was an outdoorsy
tomboy who could amply take care of herself. Even a
couple of advances from Mike the feral hadn't fazed her.
That said, it was hard to imagine Mike really intimidating
anyone. With a downturned mouth, rough, scabby fur and
a face shaped, in the words of my friend Will, 'like he'd
swallowed a saucer', his appearance seemed to sum up all
the woes of being homeless in David Cameron's Britain.

If anything, I was actually looking forward to moving
Roscoe away from here. The house was next to a main
road, but the tall fence I'd had built almost a decade
before and several years of thick ivy growth on that side
of the building meant that it was extremely difficult for

cats to get to the tarmac. Besides, The Bear, Shipley and Ralph had long since worked out that all the interesting stuff was on the non-road side of the house. However, during the place's recent makeover, I'd cut down the ivy in order to paint the fence and the bathroom window frame, which meant that it was now possible for a cat as small as Roscoe to squeeze through the bars onto the driveway. The night after I'd finished chopping the ivy back, I'd been up there to put the bin out and found her and Mike sitting a few yards away from each other, in worrying proximity to the road: two cats from different planets, Business Cat and Wino Cat, involved in some kind of arcane stare-off. My attempt the next day to block the gaps off with chicken wire proved unsuccessful. When Roscoe wanted to get somewhere, she made it happen. She was that kind of cat.

With this in mind, the move could not come quickly enough.

Where had Mike come from? I had one theory, which involved the ivy itself. Mike was actually just the latest in a succession of ginger cats to have visited us over the last couple of years, all of whom had been feral, all of whom had proved costly in an emotional and/or financial sense, and all of whom seemed initially to have emerged from the ever-expanding area where the ivy was located. I'd asked all of my close neighbours, and nobody seemed to know the origin of any of these cats. I'd come to see them as being a little like the slayers in the TV show *Buffy the Vampire Slayer*: there could only be one in the area at any one time but, as soon as one died, a replacement arrived. Sometimes, though, there was an administrative error and you got two at the same time.

The first of the ginger strays had been Graham. Moon-faced and with fur that spoke of a life of hard knocks, Graham had begun making his night-time raids on the house in early 2011, during which he would steal biscuits and then take a large piss either on the blackboard in the kitchen or the W to X section of my LP collection. After many months of trying, Gemma and I managed to 'befriend' him (ie, block off the cat flap when he was in the house) and, with the hope of either adopting him ourselves or fobbing him off onto my mum and dad, took him to the vet's and had him castrated, tested for feline AIDS and inoculated against various cat diseases. Not long after this, he'd escaped, which had left us feeling sad, and also not unlike some kind of charity for feral cat testicles. He did return a couple of times, but only to take a retaliatory piss on my Bill Withers albums, and had not been seen since spring this year.

The permanent departure of Graham had no doubt been hastened by the arrival of Alan, the Eliza Dushku to his Sarah Michelle Gellar: a cockier, more physically intimidating cat, who was better at talking to strangers and with whom Graham would often fight. The story of Alan had a happy ending, since he was now looking sumptuously upholstered and living in luxury next door with Deborah and David and their elderly female cat, Biscuit (a fellow ginger, who'd spent much of the last decade coldly rebuffing a series of polite romantic advances from The Bear). 'Oh, Alan!' I'd often hear Deborah shout, which sounded like she was reprimanding an insurance broker who'd let her down in some way, but usually just meant that Alan had done a big piss in one of her shoes.

There was a brief lull in feral activity during this period, before the arrival of another stray whom Gemma and I referred to as 'Basil Bogbrush'. This sour-faced, wiry-haired creature only hung around for a fortnight or so, and our relationship with him stalled at the first hurdle. That is to say, Gemma and I walked down to the supermarket and bought him some cooked turkey chunks – 'They're the same ones my brother has on his sandwiches!' remarked Gemma, somewhat taken aback at my extravagant choice – then threw some of them gently in his direction, in response to which he growled at me like an irate honey badger and walked off. He was almost instantly replaced by Mike, who, despite having the appearance of a cat you'd find spoiling for a fight after trying to bum a cigarette off you outside your local Costcutter, was actually very sweet. I was keen to find Mike a proper home, and Gemma and I had seemed to be getting somewhere in winning his trust up to the point when, about four weeks ago, he'd vanished.

As with Graham, I blamed myself for Mike's disappearance. I'd last set eyes on him about a week after I'd cut the ivy in the messy, straggly moments of the final party to be held at the Upside Down House. Seventies Pat, our friends Dan and Amy and I had been taking turns to sing rock anthems in my living room and I'd turned to see Mike at the window, forlornly staring in at us. I was suddenly struck by a wave of middle-class guilt, looking at his pitiful face and standing in my warm house, surrounded by empty beer cans, records and the debris of an abandoned game of Trivial Pursuit. I'd gone out to say hello to him, but Pat, Dan and Amy had called me back in, as it was my turn on the microphone, and 'Long, Long Way from Home' by Foreigner was all cued up and ready to go. What followed was an extremely painful, overreaching rendition, even by my normal tone-deaf standards. By the time it was over, and I'd had the chance to root around the food cupboard for some treats for Mike and return outside, he had vanished, and the night hung heavy and silent. He had wanted to know what love was and, selfishly, I'd been too busy singing to show him. Now, a few weeks on, I was starting to face the fact that he might be gone for ever: not the first cat I'd lost, but almost certainly the first one I'd lost via karaoke.

It had taken two full days of sawing, chopping and pulling to get rid of all the ivy. I listened to *New Yorker* magazine podcasts and shuffled songs on my iPod to keep the tedium at bay. During day two, the shuffle function arrived at 'Ivy, Ivy', a haunting song by the 1960s baroque pop group The Left Banke. I'd never known why it was called 'Ivy, Ivy' before, but now I worked it out – it was because all ivy is a massive shithead, and all ivy has even more ivy underneath it, which is even more of a massive shithead. 'Forget guns and bombs,' I thought, as I hacked at the knotted, throttling limbs and choked on their dust fumes. 'If I ever need to protect myself from an advancing army, I'll just cover myself completely in ivy.' As I began to get down to the last layer, my forearms scratched to ribbons, there was a temptation to hack more and more exuberantly, but I restrained myself, careful to look where I was cutting, still convinced of the ginger cat nest I was poised to uncover. In the end, though, all I found was an old golf trolley and a few old beer bottles, no doubt thrown over the fence by local revellers back in the rowdy summer of 2006.

The Bear, standing above me on the balcony, came over and watched with particular interest during the closing stages of the job. There was that look in his eyes again, the one that said: *I know all your secrets*. Except now it was more intense than ever. For him, Ralph, Shipley and Roscoe, what my house improvements essentially amounted to was a gradual destruction of all their favourite hang-out spots. As well as the ivy, there was the tilted, rotting shed, upon which each of them had liked to urinate, now smashed down and burned by me, with the help of David and David's biggest mallet. Then there was the hole in the boiler room wall – always such a point of fascination for Ralph, and now sadly filled in. Even Hotel Catifornia had become the victim of heartless redevelopers during the packing process. Near unrecognisable from its former cosy, welcoming state, it now contained some pottery, three old table tennis bats and a file of tax receipts from 2007.

I left the two most arduous jobs until the last minute:

clearing out the loft and the American-style crawl space beneath the house, both of which, in archetypal loft and crawl space fashion, were comprised of one per cent genuine valuables and 99 per cent junk I'd told myself I should hold onto just in case I ever needed them, even though it was patently obvious I never again would. In what 'just in case' scenario, for example, had I thought I'd need half an old broken vacuum cleaner? Just in case I suddenly discovered I'd become an entirely different person and made robots out of broken vacuum cleaner halves? How did a human – a not especially materialistic human, without children, at that – accumulate so much *stuff* in less than four decades? My adult life seemed to be separated into two distinct chunks: the first relatively brief one, where I was keen to gather possessions, in the view that they made me more of a person, and the subsequent lengthier one in which, having realised they didn't, I'd been doing my best to jettison them. Recently I'd being travelling to my local charity shop and household waste recycling centre so often, I'd started to go to other, more distant charity shops and household waste recycling centres just to shake things up a bit. When the crawl space was finally clear, and I'd banged my head on its hard, knobbly roof for the last time, I breathed such a huge sigh of relief that I let my guard down, enabling Ralph to scuttle past me and achieve a decade-long ambition by descending into its furthest recesses. As he ventured into a part of the crawl space far too narrow for me to have ever explored, the echoing 'RAAAAAAaaaallllph!' he let out somehow sounded like a Charlton-Heston-in-*Planet-of-the-Apes* cry of pain: a lament for the cruelty of humans, or at least for this new hidey-hole which was to be snatched away from him less than forty-eight hours after he'd discovered it.

Half an hour later, after I'd coaxed Ralph out of the crawl space, I took my final stroll around the garden with him and the other cats. Shipley, Ralph and Roscoe always seemed to burst into life whenever Gemma or I came outside. Shipley, especially, had a sixth sense about it, somehow knowing, from a sleeping position somewhere deep in the house's bowels, that I was in the garden, and instantly appeared alongside me to box the back of my legs and call me names. In what now constituted a rare privilege, we were joined by The Bear, who typically tended to keep his outdoor activities combined to the balcony and a window ledge next door which provided a direct view of Biscuit's favourite sleeping spot. Ralph rolled about in a patch of sunlight, Shipley hurtled down the sloping lawn, his momentum taking him all the way to the top of the apple tree at the end, and Roscoe danced about in his wake, before becoming distracted and heading off to the hedgerow to inspect some blackberries, perhaps having mistaken them for the electronic kind on which you could check your email.

The Bear scuttled down last, keeping his distance from the other cats, but showing impressive speed for a pensioner. He refrained from following Shipley up the tree, preferring instead to unleash a jet of hot yellow urine against its trunk. Beneath this tree was buried Janet, a large fluffy black male cat who, prior to his demise from a heart attack a few years ago, had been another intellectually inferior tormentor of The Bear and one of Shipley's most persuasive early influences. As The Bear dampened the bark, he stared straight at me and widened his eyes just a fraction. Was this a final, typically wry and Bearlike gesture of revenge on his old adversary? Perhaps.

Surveying the garden and those surrounding it for the final time, it struck me that this small Norfolk hillside was a patchwork of cat history. There was Janet's tree, which Janet and Shipley had so loved to climb together. Moving all the way down to the bottom of the hill, there was the rotting jetty at the edge of the lake, from which The Bear and I had once rescued a turtle who'd got itself trapped in the structure's wire meshing. Below this was the murky water from which, for some bizarre reason known only to himself, Janet had obsessively fished old sweet wrappers and crisp packets. Moving back up the hill we reached the pampas grass where, not all that long ago, Ralph, in one of his more optimistic moments, had attempted to hunt a muntjac deer. Beyond that, off to the right, was the run that held Deborah and David's six chickens, all so mysteri-ously feared by the normally swaggering Shipley that, whenever he ran past them, he made a frantic wibbling noise, which seemed to translate as 'Shit shit shit shit shit shit'. Turning sharp left, you reached the former site of the feral ivy nest; the mouldy deckchair cushion that I'd left out for Graham, then Mike, and still couldn't quite bring myself to throw away; the cypress bush under which Ralph had once sat beside a hedgehog for a whole afternoon; the gap in the hedge where Alan made his escapes, in his and Ralph's epic duels; the window The Bear smeared with his cat snot while gazing in at Biscuit. There was no denying it: this was a place with a strong cat theme. It probably shouldn't have mattered to me that it remained a place with a strong cat theme, since, after I'd moved the last of my possessions in three days' time, I would almost certainly not be coming back here ever again, but it did. When my initial buyers had announced that they weren't fond of pets, I'd felt a small cold space open up in my chest. This house had caused me a lot of stress, but that didn't mean I didn't want it to be happy when I was gone, and the idea of it being happy seemed synonymous with the idea of it being filled with four-legged life. I couldn't imagine Alan and Biscuit without nemesis cats – or, at the very least, other, lesser furry creatures – next door, to help define them; couldn't imagine the kind and thoughtful Deborah and David living next door to non-animal lovers. And what about poor Mike, in the unlikely event that he did decide to come back?

I had been enormously relieved to find out that my replacement buyers were cat lovers. Naturally, I briefed them about Mike. Even if I hadn't wanted to do it for Mike's benefit, it seemed like one of those things you do out of courtesy when you sell a house: you inform the people moving in about the best takeaways nearby, the nicest country walks, the nearest doctor, the code to the burglar alarm and the local nest of feral ginger cats.

It pained me to think about Mike, or even Graham, still being out there somewhere after I'd gone, but I couldn't afford to dwell on that: I'd drawn the line now. Besides, I'd arguably already let the needs of cats detain me at this house a year or so longer than I should have.

With the note to the new owners written, and all but

the last few things boxed up, I made my way through the cardboard jungle to bed in the house for the second to last time. The Bear padded along campily behind me. I was due to be up in five hours, but I didn't set an alarm. There were enough noisy cats here. I knew I could rely on them. Sooner or later, one would meow his own name, or call me a dreadful swear word, and I'd know it was time to make a start on moving my life to a new place.

Between solicitor stress, packing, shedding possessions and my obsessive, manic house-hunting expeditions over the last few weeks, I'd still not managed to find the one good solid night's sleep that might lift me out of the same state of absent-mindedness that had caused me to pour destructive alien liquid into an automobile I didn't own. So it was perhaps no surprise that the first thing I did, after getting into my hired van in the depot the following morning, was drive it straight into the car it was parked beside. I blame extreme tiredness for this, but in a bigger way, I blame the van hire company themselves, who, after talking me into upgrading to the biggest van I was eligible to drive (a van I made clear to them was much bigger than any I'd ever driven in the past), handed the keys to me without offering to get the van out of the extremely tight spot it had been parked in. I spent the whole journey back to my house cursing my exhaustion for making me less assertive and failing to ask for the van to be moved. The scrape on its wing was barely noticeable, but I'd really crunched the Vauxhall Zafira that had been parked next to it. I didn't know what the damage would amount to, financially speaking, but I suspected – rightly, as it later transpired – that, in one moment of idiocy, every penny I'd saved by not using a removal firm had been frittered away. I wondered if the best thing to do before I next saw my mum in a couple of days would be to write down her 'what did I tell you?' lecture and hand it to her, just to save her the hassle of delivering it to me.

After another sixty-mile round trip, during which I loaded and unloaded a van full of stuff on my own, I was, to say the least, grateful for the arrival early that afternoon of Seventies Pat.

'All right, dude?' Pat said, handing me a six-pack of lager as I opened the front door to him. Six foot two and a half in his snakeskin cowboy boots, he represented a reassuring if somewhat unlikely moving-day spectacle, his long blond hair, cravat and corduroy bell-bottoms rippling slightly in the autumn breeze. A few of my friends favoured clothes from the middle of the last century, but Pat was the only one you never found off duty. I'd not had the privilege of seeing his nightwear, but I suspected that even his pyjamas were made from crushed velvet and had a slight flare to them. His reputation for rock dandyism preceded him in his native Black Country, to the extent that recently, during a routine transaction involving a pasty in the Dudley branch of Gregg's the bakers, the cashier, who he'd never met before, had paused and looked him over for a couple of seconds, then asked, 'Are yow Seventies Pat?' – to which Pat had replied, 'Yep.'

The plan was that Pat and I would shift the rest of my

stuff unaccompanied, over the next two days, before Gemma, who was back in the West Country for work, arrived to assist with the unpacking. Pat was helping me out of the kindness of his big corduroy heart, his only payment being a brace of Indian takeaways and a couple of original LPs by the 1970s Irish folk group Planxty I'd picked up for him the previous week in Norwich, but he did have an ulterior motive. Pat had never been a cat owner himself, but possessed a serious soft spot for Ralph, in whom he recognised a kindred spirit. I knew Pat would never attempt to steal Ralph, but it was an unspoken fact between me, him and Gemma that, should Gemma and I perish unexpectedly, Ralph would go to live with Pat in Dudley. Once there, the two of them would live the life the Lord intended them to: waxing their sideburns together in front of his 'n' his mirrors while listening to a T. Rex album before heading out to hog the jukeboxes and pool tables of the Black Country's finest real ale pubs, as an assortment of leather-clad rock chicks looked on admiringly. We wouldn't be taking the cats until our final journey to the bungalow in a couple of days, but it was established very quickly that, when the four of them were divided up for the journey, Ralph would be travelling in Pat's car, not in the van with me.

'I'll let you take The Bear,' said Pat. 'I love that little dude, but he freaks me out, the way he stares at me. I feel like he's planning something.'

Pat's fear turned out to be a self-fulfilling prophecy when, the following morning, I arrived in the living room to find Pat standing beside the sofa bed on which he'd slept the previous night, inspecting a large vomit stain.

'All roight, now listen,' said Pat. 'I just want to make one thing clear straight away: it wasn't me who did that.'

Behind us on the windowsill sat The Bear, looking the opposite way and cleaning a paw. There was something a little bit forced about the way he did it, suggesting that, were we to check, we'd find that his paw hadn't actually needed cleaning at all.

'It's OK,' I said. 'It's probably just one last protest before we leave.'

'I can't believe he had time to do it,' said Pat. 'I only went into the bathroom long enough to have a slash and spray myself with Old Spice.'

'Yeah, he can still move quickly when he needs to.'

On the whole, I had been very impressed at the way The Bear had dealt with the few days immediately prior to the move. There had been none of the last-minute disappearing acts or desolate *meeoop*ing sessions that had characterised previous relocations. Instead, he seemed watchful and curious, always keen to keep an eye on the action but never seeming quite to disapprove of it. I even caught him climbing the ladder after me and trying to get into the loft at one point, which made me wonder if those house-hunting worries about staircases were a little premature. When I finally fed him into his cat carrier, he felt soft and compliant, rather than rigid and stubborn, as he always had at these moments in the past. I took his sanguine attitude as further confirmation that I was doing the right thing.

Of course, it could be argued that each of us still had unfinished business here. I'd never got around to building that writing shed I'd often talked about, or getting the goat I'd always wanted for the garden and, despite many efforts, The Bear had never melted Biscuit's icy heart, but we were both men of the world now, old enough to realise that life was never going to be a perfect To Do list on which you managed to tick all the boxes.

'Don't worry – we'll be there in no time,' I said as I started the van for the final journey to the bungalow, with The Bear and Roscoe belted in in their carriers on the two passenger seats behind me, but my reassurance was superfluous; the two of them were amazingly placid. Following behind us in Pat's car were its owner and Ralph: Seventies Pat and his Seventies Cat. Behind them were my mum and dad, who'd driven down at the last minute from Nottinghamshire to give me some much-needed assistance cleaning the house, with the very last of the boxes, one of which contained Shipley.

'THIS CAT IS A GOBSHITE,' said my dad, emerging from the car with Shipley, on reaching the bungalow. 'HE WOULDN'T SHUT UP ALL THE WAY HERE. I'M SURE HE CALLED ME A WAZZOCK AT ONE POINT. IS HE ALWAYS LIKE THAT?'

'Pretty much,' I said. 'Haven't you noticed before? Then again, I suppose you've only known him for twelve years.'

'DON'T BE FOOKIN' CHEEKY, YOU LANKY STREAK OF PISS. I DON'T ALWAYS REMEMBER THINGS. SEE IF YOU REMEMBER THINGS WHEN YOU'RE SIXTY-FOUR AND YOU'VE BEEN UP SINCE FIVE.'

For the time being, I installed the cats in the spare bedroom with some food and water. The water was split between a dish and The Bear's favourite watering can, which I'd brought inside and placed on a sheet of newspaper in the hope that its presence might comfort him. Each of the cats took turns to do that thing cats always do in a new house, where they seem to be checking all the walls for secret passageways and weak spots, but none of them seemed unusually agitated. I would keep them in for a few days, but probably not much longer. I was massively grateful that they'd been so well behaved throughout the move, since a last-minute feline-based panic would probably have been the thing that pushed events over the line separating 'sketchily organised stress fest' from 'all-out disaster'. My decision to upgrade to the biggest van possible had turned out to be a small wise decision wrapped up inside a much larger unwise one: even with all that space, my recent pruning of possessions and Pat's ace packing skills, we required seven journeys there and back in the van, stretched over three days, meaning I got it back to the depot with only moments to spare. Without us both working non-stop from the moment we woke up each day to the moment we dropped at night, the emergency arrival of my mum and dad and a little more help from my friends Drew and Andy, we wouldn't have managed it.

'Pat's such a good pal, isn't he, lending you a hand like that,' my mum remarked later. 'But I thought you said he was a big bloke. He didn't seem all that big to me.' Her comment said a lot about the state the move had left the two of us in: bedraggled, rain-lashed, windswept and crooked-backed. Pat might have made the sensible change from his cowboy boots into an old pair of Converse, but it was moving itself that had rendered him temporarily reduced in size. Afterwards, he and I agreed that we felt less like we'd hired a van than been repeatedly reversed over by one. As we leaned on the outside wall after it was all over, surrounded by broken lamp shards, comparing our bruises, we felt all of our combined seventy-nine and a half years.

'I was thinking,' said Pat, taking a much-needed swig of Peroni. 'It's a good job you didn't get that goat.'

If anything, the steamrollered feeling became even more extreme the following day, when everyone had gone. I was limping slightly from slipping on some wet leaves while carrying a heavy plant pot the previous afternoon, I could feel a cold coming on, my head felt like someone had jammed it full of old cotton wool and lint in the night and every time I turned around, my hip made an odd, tiny clicking sound, like I'd left a loose button somewhere in the bone's cavity. After all the work of the last few months, a sensible person would probably have taken the opportunity to spend the day in bed recovering but, not being a sensible person, I chose instead to climb a ladder and put twenty-five heavy boxes of books and old magazines in the loft, assemble two large items of flat-pack furniture, then go straight out into Norwich and, accompanied by my friend Louise and some strangers, drink five pints of beer on an empty stomach. My main memory of the hours after that are of being carried aloft through Norwich city centre by two people I'd met just two hours previously, then getting woken up first thing the next morning by a carpenter who, in a rare moment of thoughtful planning, I'd booked to fit my new microchip cat flap. The carpenter was polite enough not to comment on my appearance, though he must have been slightly confused, since Halloween was still a full week and a half away.

Physically, I felt even worse than the day before but, as I said goodbye to the carpenter, this was offset by a gradually dawning relief: my old house, such a millstone to me for so long, was sold, the new one was in a passable state for when Gemma arrived back from Devon the following day, the cats would soon be going out and exploring and I could at last permit myself to relax. I'd just empty the cat litter, I decided, then head back to bed with a book.

People talk the big talk about uranium and lead but, as anyone who's ever bagged it up knows, the world's heaviest substance is actually used cat litter. This is generally OK if you're feeling strong and have a hard-wearing bin liner, but somewhat less OK if, like me on this particular morning, you were feeling about as tough as a newborn foal and had just lazily grabbed a value Morrisons refuse sack that you'd previously used to transport some cushions in a house move. The next twenty-five seconds played out like some kind of 'What Not To Do When You've Just Moved House With Cats' public information video, the only missing bits being the giant neon flashing exclamation marks as each of my mistakes occurred: the open door left behind me as I walked barefoot across the drive; the bag splitting and spilling its contents; Shipley shooting through the gap behind me, me diving for him, missing and ripping a strip of skin off my arm on the cold, wet concrete; the door blowing shut behind me; the terror on my face as I heard the click of its Yale lock and felt in the pocket of my pyjama bottoms for a non-existent key.

Being 'the new person with four cats', I'd hoped to be able to present myself for the first time to my next-door neighbour in a respectable sort of way, and so turning up on her doorstep clad only in pyjama bottoms and an old, ripped Tom Petty and The Heartbreakers T-shirt telling wild-eyed tales of a lost feline wasn't exactly what you'd call ideal. I was, however, fortunate on two counts: first, Vivian, who lived in the house to the left of the bunga-low, was at home in my hour of need; second, she was extremely kind, putting the kettle on, offering me a towel to dry my feet, letting me borrow her landline to call a locksmith and lending me some shoes. Due to go out shortly, she even trustingly offered to let me stay in her house on my own while I waited for a stranger to come and break into mine, but, feeling I'd imposed more than enough already, I declined, thanked her for her hospital-ity and trudged back in the direction of the waste ground I'd seen Shipley heading towards.

To be honest, I wasn't overly worried about Shipley. I knew him well enough to understand that he was very unlikely to get lost, even in a new outdoor habitat. As my resident public relations cat, he would be only too keen to get back to his new central office and catch up on cor-respondence. Sure enough, after a couple of whistles and an encouraging but slightly nervous responding profanity,

I located him cowering behind a broken fence panel, scooped him up and headed back to the front door. Vivian, it turned out, had relatively large feet and, though her shoes were a couple of sizes too small for me, I found that I could walk in them easily enough. I wondered about taking them off before the locksmith arrived but, on further consideration, decided against it. It looked like it was about to rain and, within the context of the indignities of the last few days, the idea of a potentially manly stranger seeing me wearing pyjamas and the shoes of a woman twenty-five years my senior didn't really seem that much of a big deal.

I'd not programmed Shipley's microchip number into the cat flap as yet, so the two of us hunkered down on the concrete, out of the wind. Shipley soon got comfortable in his favourite upside-down position on my lap and began a possessive, industrial purr. After ten minutes, a tabby cat I'd never seen before – lean, short-haired and muscular – prowled into the driveway and began to sniff some of the scattered cat litter. I called to him, but in language even Shipley deemed shocking, he told me to get lost then jogged off in the direction of Vivian's front garden. A couple of minutes after that, the rain started, and all there was left for us to do was wait.

# Ten Short Conversations I Have Had With Cats

Me: 'Am I imagining it, or did you just totally blank me?'

Cat: 'No, you're not imagining it. I overheard you telling your friend that I was fat with a tiny head.'

Me: 'I meant it lovingly.'

Cat: 'I guess that's OK then.'

Me: 'I'm glad you think so.'

Cat: 'Oh, one other thing.'

Me: 'Yes?'

Cat: 'I just vomited "lovingly" inside your best cardigan.'

Cat: 'This food is total shit.'

Me: 'But you said that about the last kind, too.'

Cat: 'This is worse.'

Me: 'Is that a phone in your paw?'

Cat: 'No.'

Me: 'It totally is. It's a phone, and you're pressing the buttons with your nose! Who are you calling?'

Cat: 'Cats Protection.'

Me: 'I just went into the living room and found the chair turned upside down. Was that your work?'

Cat: 'The wind did it.'

Me: 'Bollocks.'

Cat: 'No, it's completely true. "The Wind" is my super-hero name.'

Me (stifled): 'A-choo!'

Cat: 'You just sneezed. I told you never to do that around me.'

Me: 'I'm sorry. I tried not to, but I couldn't stop it. I made sure it was quiet.'

Cat: 'Well, don't. Don't do it at all. It puts me off.'

Me: 'Puts you off what?'

Cat: 'Being a cat.'

Me: 'Your tail is in some jam.'

Cat: 'That's intentional. I like the way it feels.'

Me: 'Yeah, right. I believe you.'

Cat (leaving): 'I DON'T NEED YOU.'

Me: 'Oh, you're back.'

Cat: 'Need jellied meat.'

Me: 'I'm sorry. Did the noise of that pan lid I just put away upset your delicate ear drums in some way?'

Cat: 'It did.'

Me: 'You're kind of touchy. Did you know that?'

Cat: 'You will never understand the life of an artist, and what it entails.'

Me: 'Was that yawn you just did directed at me?'

Cat: 'No. Don't be paranoid.'

Me: 'It's just . . . it seemed kind of a comment aimed in my direction.'

Cat: 'OK. Lately I tire of you somewhat.'

Me: 'Look. I'll just go, since that seems like it will be easier for both of us.'

Cat: 'WAIT!'

Me: 'OK!'

Cat: 'Before you leave, can you get me that sweater I like to sit on?'

Me: 'Did I just hear you meowing at a shoe?'

Cat: 'Yes. It was some new performance art I was working on.'

Me: 'Oh, excellent. I'm impressed. It's good to see you working and motivated again.'

Cat: 'OMG. How gullible can you be? Of course it wasn't, you idiot. I left a dead vole in it earlier.'

Cat: 'Hi. Do you mind if I sit on you?'

Me: 'Would this be because you're covered in rain?'

Cat: 'No. That's purely a coincidence.'

Me: 'OK. Go on then.'

Cat: 'Cheers.'

Me: 'We should do this more often. It's nice.'

Cat: 'Dry now. Bye.'

Cat: 'I hate this food. I'm leaving it.'

Me: 'Here, have this one instead.'

Cat: '*Love* it.'

Me: 'Can I let you into a secret?'

Cat: 'OK. I like secrets.'

Me: 'It's the exact same bowl of food. All I did was move it.'

Cat: 'I am fire and the wind. Do not attempt to know me.'

# There is a Cat And It Never Goes Out

'WHATEVER YOU DO, DON'T BITE THAT CAT'S NECK,' said my dad. 'HE'S JUST HAD HIS FLEA TREATMENT.' Having been for a long walk in the Lincolnshire countryside, my parents and I had just arrived back in their living room, where Floyd was fast asleep on the sofa. Pressed against the window opposite him was the ghostly white face of Casper, whom my mum would soon no doubt take pity on and allow in.

I'd never shown any inclination to bite Floyd's neck but, because my dad was enthusiastic about that kind of thing, he tended to assume everyone wanted a go. Even if I had sunk my teeth into Floyd's scruff at the present moment, it's doubtful Floyd would have noticed, so far and deep into the land of sleep had he vanished. Floyd and my dad shared a lack of respect for moderation: they were either fully switched off or fully switched on at any one point. Their 'off' modes were quite similar: both

preferred to sleep on soft furniture, but could rest equally soundly on any vaguely horizontal surface that wasn't liable to draw blood. The only difference was in the vagaries of their 'on' modes. For Floyd, being 'on' meant roaming the fields surrounding their house, dry-humping Casper while putting his tongue in his ear, leaving rodent blood spatter on the Welsh dresser or – perhaps most impressive of all – playing games of fetch with a variety of objects, including a catnip mouse and an old Action Man toy. For my dad, it meant enthusing about firewood, shouting at TV weather presenters, recounting incidents from his council estate childhood or walking around the house topless while flossing his teeth and listening to African pop music at nightclub volume.

It's said that the menstrual cycles of female housemates will often synchronise, with time. Similarly, my dad's and Floyd's 'on' and 'off' phases had begun to coincide more and more frequently the longer they lived together – Floyd, for example, warming up for his first dead mouse of the evening just as my dad sank his first whisky and told the story of the time in 1962 when he and his cousin Flob tried to set their farts on fire in a field on the Nottinghamshire–Derbyshire border. Today was a rare day when man and cat were out of sync. Soon my dad would head off for his afternoon nap, while Floyd would wake up, eat a full sachet of cat food, make violent, arid love to Casper then head off hungrily into the back field.

My dad being 'on' for the last few hours had made for a typically eventful walk. Our original eight-mile route had been compromised due to the River Trent bursting its banks. Undeterred, my dad had tried to leap over the flood and ended up dropping his Ordnance Survey map and glasses in the river. At this point, with him unable to see where they'd gone, I'd waded into the shallows and rescued them just before the current had a chance to catch them and wash them away for ever. In its soggy state, the map remained just legible enough to help us navigate to the pub, where my dad immediately strode up to the barmaid and asked, 'HAVE YOU GOT ANY CHIPS?' then, after she'd answered in the affirmative, ordered a beef sandwich instead and asked her to turn the music down. We'd then squelched back to the car, my dad stopping briefly to point out the house of a man whose family had made a lot of money from manufacturing farming equipment.

'POSH PEOPLE ALWAYS LIVE LONG BECAUSE THEY'RE POSH AND DON'T HAVE ANYTHING TO WORRY ABOUT,' he observed.

'I see your point, but I don't think that's totally true,' I replied.

'No, it's not, Mick,' said my mum. 'You're making a silly generalisation.'

'THINK ABOUT IT. BAMBER GASCOIGNE. CHRISTOPHER LEE. BOTH OF THEM ARE OLD AND POSH. YOU HAVEN'T COMMENTED ON THIS FLEECE I'M WEARING.'

'No, I haven't. Sorry. Is it new?'

'YEAH. IT WAS EXPENSIVE, TOO.'

'What happened to your others?'

'I MOWED ONE BY MISTAKE AND SET FIRE TO THE OTHER DOING A BONFIRE FOR EDNA NEXT DOOR. YOU NEED A GOOD FLEECE. IT'S TIME YOU STARTED DRESSING PROPERLY.' He inspected my wide-brimmed pilgrim hat and my coat, a different item to the one that had almost caused me not to be able to rent my house, but still over ten years old. 'I'D PROBABLY CALL THE POLICE IF I LIVED IN ONE OF THESE VILLAGES AND SAW YOU WALK PAST MY HOUSE DRESSED LIKE THAT. YOU LOOK LIKE YOU SLEEP ROUGH AND STEAL CHICKENS.'

Now, a couple of hours later, having greeted Floyd with an 'All RIGHT, OUR KID?' and massaged his scruff, he led me upstairs to his office. 'HERE,' he said, reaching under his desk and handing me a large gun. 'TAKE THIS.'

It felt a bit like a rite of passage, a rural British equivalent to the kind of handover that might happen in American hill country during the early part of the previous century. A woodsman father passes a cherished weapon to a bearded son in a big hat who's come to call on him in his hour of need. The main difference here being that the gun in question did not shoot bullets but water, and was supposed to be used to scare off a cat, not to kill a toothless rival in a feud. A year earlier, when my dad had bought the gun, which was about half the length of my arm and had 'AK-47' written near its trigger, I'd been sceptical. He'd claimed its purpose had been to frighten away a neighbouring black cat who had been picking on Floyd, but I sensed it was more for his own enjoyment. I couldn't have imagined shooting it at a cat myself, but extreme situations called for extreme measures.

On the morning Shipley and I had been locked out of the bungalow and we'd met the tabby cat from down the road, I'd not found the tabby's greeting very welcoming, but even that could not have prepared me for what a holy terror he would turn out to be. In the six weeks since then, this dappled thug had mercilessly terrorised Ralph, Shipley, The Bear and Roscoe, and all my and Gemma's attempts to see him off – violently clapping our hands, for example, or shouting 'Hey! Furface! Get back to your patch!' – had come to nothing. I liked to think I loved all cats, but this one really was a dickhead: the kind of cat who, when he wasn't round here bullying my cats, probably went to a cat gym, overused Lynx deodorant in the changing rooms and constantly boasted to other cats about his pecs.

The tabby's visits were of a much more mercenary kind than those we'd witnessed from the feral gingers at the Upside Down House. If this cat was homeless, then the local cat hostel he was frequenting surely featured tip-top grooming services, a small rowing machine and nightly barbecues. Due to the impregnable shield that was the microchip cat flap, Gymcat's motives could not be put down to food. His attacks were purely about territory and ego. They also brought with them a sobering realisation about a new stage of life for Ralph and Shipley, for so long the two alpha mogs of the household. Ralph had stood up to Gymcat for a while, but, since arriving through the cat flap last week with his magnificent white bib covered in blood – some of it no doubt his oppressor's, some of it from two cuts on his own face – he'd been lying low. Shipley, meanwhile, had been looking a bit wilted ever since the move. His fur had a greyed-over dullness to it, and his pointy tail had begun to take on the appearance of the one ailing leaf you'll sometimes find hanging off an ill-watered dracaena plant.

Shipley had long ago made a bargain with me, which stated that on the condition I fed him before 6.30 a.m. he wouldn't go around the house knocking over waste-paper baskets, scratching carpets and swear-shouting. On mornings when I contravened the deadline, he remained a foul-mouthed menace, but outside the house he was now a far more nervous animal, checking the coast was clear, scuttling out to empty his bowels then rushing back in to avoid being set upon. The Bear, too, was hardly going out, though I put this down to the colder weather and his increasingly indoorsy nature. He'd even abandoned his long-adored watering can for a new arrangement, where he drank, pawed at and even talked to a bowl of water I'd placed in the bathroom. He and Roscoe seemed to be dealing with the Gymcat situation most calmly of all, but, well over a month after the move, the temporary litter tray remained regrettably in place. If you ignored the finer details, I was doing something I hadn't done for well over a decade, and something which I hadn't ever planned to do again: I was living with four indoor cats.

I'd always viewed my cats as a bit of a handful, but, stripped of their independence, they had become a much bigger one. A typical morning, for example, would unfold a little like this:

5.13 a.m. Wake up to the sound of Ralph meowing his own name and knocking stuff off shelves.

6.31 a.m. Wake up again to the sound of Shipley swearing, knocking bins over and scratching the hall carpet outside bedroom.

6.32 a.m. Let Shipley in.

6.33 a.m. Get up and head blearily to kitchen, replacing rubbish in waste-paper bins along the way.

6.44 a.m. Feed all four cats.

6.58 a.m. Throw away gribbly bits cats have left in bottom of food bowls.

7.40 a.m. Hear growling noise and, being careful to keep door on latch, rush outside in dressing gown to save Ralph from Gymcat.

9.17 a.m. Get distracted from work by mournful, ghostly wailing and rush into bathroom to find The Bear staring at bowl of water and talking to it.

9.49 a.m. Hear growling noise and, being careful to keep door on latch, rush outside in dressing gown to save Shipley from Gymcat.

10.11 a.m. Arrive in living room to find Shipley ignoring brand-new scratching post and sharpening claws on spines of four original 1960s Byrds LPs instead.

10.53 a.m. Get distracted from work by mournful, ghostly wailing and rush into bathroom to find The Bear staring at bowl of water and talking to it.

11.01 a.m. Rush across living room to stop Roscoe punching the crud out of Shipley.

11.12 a.m. See Shipley's tail. Worry about it, and feed him fresh turkey chunks from fridge.

11.14 a.m. Put turkey chunks away. See The Bear instantly arrive in kitchen. Feel bad about him not getting any earlier. Get turkey chunks out again. Remove Shipley from The Bear's face.

11.16 a.m. Empty and refill litter tray.

11.17 a.m. Walk past freshly changed litter tray and notice enormous dump already deposited in it.

    11.46 a.m. Begin to prepare cheese and tomato sandwich, watched closely by The Bear.

11.47 a.m. Rush outside to rescue Ralph from Gymcat.

11.48 a.m. Arrive back in kitchen to find Shipley and The Bear on work surface eating half-prepared cheese and tomato sandwich. Remove The Bear and Shipley from work surface. Begin sandwich again.

11.53 a.m. Step in cat vomit on way to living room with sandwich. Head into bathroom to clean foot.

11.57 a.m. Finally settle down for first meal of the day, while stared at by all four cats in cutting and accusatory fashion.

In truth, I could not blame the cats' new status as virtual hermits entirely on Gymcat. When Gemma and I had initially been to view the bungalow, we'd noticed a depot of some kind behind its back fence containing tractors and skips. Spotting a school playing field beyond the depot, I'd asked the agent showing us around – and, later, one of his colleagues – if the depot was solely connected to the upkeep of the school's outdoor area, and they'd both confirmed it was. Either they didn't actually know the truth, which was that the depot had been leased to a separate,

much busier company and had created a local noise problem, or they made the assumption that, as someone who
wore old coats, I wouldn't mind very much. Over the last
few months, Vivian next door had been in a legal battle
with the depot, which woke her every morning at 7 a.m.

with clanging noises then belched diesel fumes into our adjoining gardens for most of the day. I was a veteran of houses with serious noise issues, some of which had been far worse than this, and my status as a temporary renter lessened my worries, but the cats were scared of the depot and reluctant to go near it, even when its workforce had gone home. With the garden made entirely from concrete, their only equivalent to the vast green space they'd had at their previous home was the waste ground to the side of the house, but this was the exact place from which Gymcat made his attacks: a between-the-gardens area of gnarled trees and muddy hillocks that gained an extra air of menace thanks to the blood-curdling fox noises which rang out from it almost every night. 'What does the fox say?' asked the irritating yet strangely compelling song 'The Fox' by the novelty technopop group Ylvis, a hit of the moment. Awake at night listening to these fearsome noises, I would ask myself the same question. I narrowed the answer down to the following:

1. 'Hi. I am your new neighbour. I would like to eat one of your cats. The small black and white one who resembles a living cartoon looks especially delicious.'

2. 'I am mad as hell about centuries of persecution by Britain's ruling class and I'm not going to take it any more. Woe betide any other creature who crosses my path.'

3. 'I am a fox. I enjoy performing taboo, often somewhat violent acts with other foxes and,

well, pretty much any animal I can find, to be
honest. It's fun, and provides a much-needed
temporary distraction in the current anti-fox climate perpetuated by the *Daily Mail* and the
Conservative government.'

There wasn't much I could do about the fox or depot problems for now, but I could at least make an attempt to deal
with Gymcat. He was amazingly cunning, though, perhaps due to the time he spent in bushy-tailed company,
and I knew I'd have to be ready for him. On the evening
I returned from seeing my parents, I'd taken all the necessary precautions, leaving the door on the latch for quick
opening, filling the gun's cartridge and waiting quietly in
the utility room with its light and the kitchen's off but the
outside floodlight on. In retrospect, it probably would have
been better if I'd told Gemma exactly what I was doing.
It's always going to be a bit worrying when, looking for
your boyfriend to ask if he wants to come and join you to
watch an episode of a sitcom, you find him pressed against
a wall in a darkened corner of the house cradling a firearm.
However, after I explained my plan, her concern began to
diminish at least slightly. A few minutes later, Shipley,
giving me a quizzical look on the way, stepped gingerly out
of the cat flap and, like clockwork, a minute after that I
heard a *screeeawwwgh* noise.

Everything about what I did next was just right: I was
swift yet soundless on my feet, springing through the door
and landing in front of Gymcat before he knew what had
happened. What I hadn't anticipated was a problem with

my weapon. I'd seen the giant water pistol in action the previous Christmas, when my dad and two of my cousins had got tipsy and started shooting it at each other, but I hadn't remembered a flaw in its design: when you pulled the trigger, it began to make a rattling fake machine-gun noise before the water squirted from the end of it. I was no expert in weaponry, but this seemed to defeat the object somewhat. You didn't get, say, hand grenades that, as you sent them on their way, sang a little song about being a hand grenade. By the time some water had actually shot out of the water pistol, the enemy was long gone.

Gymcat was, by some distance, the most frustrating neighbour cat I'd ever encountered. Mike and his ginger predecessors had nothing on him for stealth or elusiveness. My initial attempts to befriend him had resulted in the coldest furry shoulder I'd ever been on the end of, and his responses to my attempts to scare him off were received in the most infuriating manner: he never let me get close to him, yet, as soon as he was a safe distance away, he'd resume his cock of the walk swagger, and it was never too long before he was back. With the water pistol idea a non-starter, I racked my brain for an alternative. The house had no upstairs, so there was no way of ambushing him from above with a mug of water, and he was too quick for me to have any success with my attempt to splash him from ground level.

'I wish my mum and dad's dog was here,' said Gemma. 'I'd get him to punch him. He punches everyone. He punched one of their binmen last week.'

On the day the cats and I had taken our last stroll

around the garden of the Upside Down House, it had still felt almost like summer, but a few days later Pat and I had moved the last of our furniture to the bungalow in cold, driving rain under a big black sky which had never properly gone away. A darkness seemed to envelop the building, exacerbated by the reign of Gymcat, the ominous clang of the depot and the respiratory illness Gemma had been suffering from. In a sense, it felt as if we'd moved the cats not just to a new house, but to winter itself. One day, with a howling gale blowing outside, I opened the door to the postman who, handing me a small pile of mail, noticed a name that wasn't mine on an envelope at the top and said, 'Oops, that one isn't for you. That's for the man who lived here before and died.'

A few days later, in even higher winds, the back fence blew down, leaving us feeling more like we were in the depot than merely next to it. I couldn't blame Ralph when, the following day, he chose to take refuge up the chimney. At first we hadn't known that Ralph was up the chimney, and had been genuinely worried about him for several hours, with me even going so far as to look for him inside the skips and the open cab of a tractor in the depot. Having searched in what we thought was every conceivable place, we were sitting anxiously in the living room wringing our hands over what to do next when a cat not dissimilar to Ralph, except all black in colour, crashed down into the unused fireplace in front of us. 'Perhaps he was looking for Cat Santa?' said Gemma, as we washed the soot off him in the bath a few minutes later. It was a good theory, but I knew it wasn't true:

Ralph had simply been searching for the magic portal leading back to the kinder, warmer, greener place we had arrived here from.

At around the same time I moved to the bungalow, a friend of mine, Jane, had moved with her two cats, Rick and Dolly, from a suburban house backing on to woodland to a small gardenless London flat. Just after Christmas, following a meal and a few drinks out in London, Seventies Pat, Gemma and I were invited over to check out her new place. In pride of place in Jane's new living room, dwarfing everything around it, stood the biggest feline-related guilt purchase I'd ever seen: a towering edifice which strived to combine the merits of a scratching post, a furry maze and the Empire State Building and did a pretty good job of pulling it off. 'It took me a whole day to construct it,' said Jane. 'Obviously, they both completely ignore it. I'm training them to use the toilet, though, and they're doing pretty well at that.'

'You mean, a litter tray?' I asked. 'Have they not used one before?'

'No, I mean the actual toilet.'

Right on cue, Seventies Pat, who had disappeared two minutes earlier, emerged from the bathroom. On his left foot was one of the two cowboy boots he'd been wearing when he went in there. In his right hand was the other cowboy boot, its heel caked in litter-flecked cat excrement. 'Er, roight, we've got a bit of a situation here,' he said.

Ten minutes later, after Jane had cleaned up the mess, we all sat down with a cup of tea. 'Sorry,' she told Pat. 'It's not your fault. I should have mentioned earlier that I was training them: the way it works is that the litter tray sits on the toilet seat and you have to move it if you want to go for a wee. But Rick and Dolly miss sometimes and the poo ends up on the floor.' She shook her head. 'Oh, I don't know. Maybe it's not going to work after all.' She bent to stroke Dolly, who was crouching under the coffee table, looking a little nervous. 'It's all been a big change for them, becoming indoor cats, but hopefully they'll settle down soon.'

'I think if I was a cat, I'd be an indoor cat,' said Pat, who, on both of the occasions he'd been on country walks with me, had turned up wearing cowboy boots, a leather patchwork jacket and a cravat.

Pat and I had many things in common, but this was most assuredly not one of them. I knew I could never be an indoor cat and, unlike Jane, whose work demanded a home near central London, I had no actual need to be one. A few months living in a city, surrounded by con-crete – even a small, gentle city, where greenery was never too far away – had confirmed to me just what a lover of fresh air and tranquillity I was. The countryside wasn't just something I liked, it was part of me, and always had been. And what about the poor cats? When they were feeling cooped up, unlike me they didn't have the advantage of being able to go out and walk around the former site of an Iceni village or through a haunted forest past the ivy-strangled ruin of a Saxon church to a decaying clifftop. They couldn't even get as far as next door's hedge without being pounced on by the feline version of Biff from *Back to the Future*. I was starting to see the same look about them that I'd seen about Rick and Dolly: a little light had faded from their eyes, a little lustre from their fur.

An indoor cat was safe from roads and predators, but what was lost at the same time? What heroic hunting expeditions? What kinglike feelings from the top of an enthusiastically climbed tree? What perfect afternoons languidly cleaning a paw on a freshly mown lawn's most prestigious sun-patterned corner? Safety was no good if its tariff was a radically diminished experience of life's wonder. When a happy person or pet dies young, we don't just say 'At least they lived a full, happy life' because we're trying to console ourselves; we do so because we know, in our heart of hearts, that this is more important than anything.

Up in north Nottinghamshire, Floyd – a cat if ever there was one who enjoyed flooring the pedal of life's throttle – was experiencing his first proper taste of snow. He was evidently enjoying this, particularly the opportunity it provided to seriously mess up the futures of some cold, wet mice. 'He got a bit overenthusiastic yesterday, forgot where the garden pond was and did a big leap straight into it,' my mum told me over the din of Radio Four, which my dad had on at a painfully high volume upstairs.

'He got very wet but he was soon out again, bounding about. I heard your dad letting him out the other day and telling him to watch out for fookwits and loonies, but I think maybe it's the fookwits and loonies he should be telling to watch out for Floyd. His kill count has gone up to three per night.

'I used to have some lovely relaxing mornings to myself before we had a cat, when your dad used to go swimming with Malcolm, but now I spend most of them cleaning blood spatter off the walls and having to listen to the *Today* programme at full blast.'

'WHAT'S THAT?' shouted my dad, from upstairs. 'ARE YOU TALKING ABOUT ME? DID YOU KNOW PAMELA ANDERSON FROM *BAYWATCH* IS MAR-RIED TO BILLY CONNOLLY NOW? SHE'S A PSYCHIATRIST THESE DAYS.'

'Floyd's still very lovely, in a lot of ways,' continued my mum. 'He's not the cat he was, though. He's got a life away from us now. He'll be out for hours, then if he wants feeding when he comes back in the night he'll stick one of his claws in my nostril to wake me up. He's clever and he knows it works. I worry that there's been a change in his and Casper's relationship, too. He's always been the dominant partner, but he might be getting a bit *too* dom-inant. Casper looks quite bedraggled a lot of the time.'

I'd had a welcome break from bloodstains recently – there had been no rodent slaughter at the bungalow – and I'd never much fancied a nostril piercing, let alone one performed by a cat, but strangely, in spending a couple of days with my parents and Floyd and Casper, I became more aware of a part of cat ownership I'd lost recently and found myself mourning it. As I watched Floyd bolt across the snowy lawn in pursuit of a camouflaged Casper, I felt a vicarious jealousy on behalf of my own cats, now under house arrest. My dad's warning to Floyd was superfluous. There were no fookwits and loonies here. These two cats lived charmed lives, in Cat Paradise.

A dark January in Norfolk became an even darker February, and the caring folks at the letting agency continued to ignore my requests for the garden fence to be mended. Then one morning Gemma carried a plate of toast into the living room to find a woman in a hard hat and a fluorescent tabard standing in our flower bed, smoking a cigarette and staring defiantly at her as if to say, 'What do you think you're doing in your own house, carrying a plate of toast?' But Gemma had not been able to make this truly her house: recurring health problems had kept her tied to her trusted doctor in Devon and made a proper, committed search for work in Norfolk impossible. On the journeys I'd made west to drop her off or collect her, I'd fallen more in love than ever with Devon. Its wildest parts had a wildness I'd not experienced anywhere I'd lived. I felt intoxicatingly at home walking on its moors and high clifftop paths. It struck me as a county that a person could get uniquely, magically lost in. A few months before, I'd not been in a position financially, or in terms of transport, to move there easily, but since then I'd got a troublesome mortgage off my hands and published a successful book. I even had a car again to use for house-hunting. There was always a chance I'd ruin it by putting the wrong kind of liquid in its engine, but that was less likely now: I wasn't as tired as I had been, and I had others looking out for me, such as my dad, who had taken it upon himself to add his own makeshift label to the filler cap while I wasn't looking.

Gemma and I had held a housewarming party of sorts just before Christmas, but even at that point, our imminent future was becoming clear and, for all the night's dancing and excitable chatter, the atmosphere was if anything more redolent of a housecooling party. Shipley had always seemed to enjoy the presence of large groups of drunk people in the Upside Down House, and was often to be found standing in the middle of them, offering loud and candid opinions on a variety of subjects, or wading into games of Giant Jenga with cataclysmic results, but now he sulked in the bedroom with Ralph, The Bear and Roscoe. The Bear had never been a big one for my parties, which featured what he surely viewed as a criminal absence of Morrissey records, but he did emerge briefly at this one to adjudicate morally on some of the night's most dramatic events. I missed this adjudication, but was filled in on some of it later by Seventies Pat.

At around 3 a.m., when most of the other guests had left, Pat had found himself in the kitchen with Nicci, a friend of mine from many years ago when I'd been a music journalist. Ever since they'd met about three months earlier, a flirtation had been simmering between Pat, who had just come out of a long-term relationship, and Nicci, who was still in one, just about. To all who'd witnessed their interactions from any distance, it was clear they were smitten with each other. Until now, they'd managed to restrain themselves from taking things any further, but, finally alone, after an evening of suggestive nudges and spiced rum, Pat bent and as he inched his lips closer to Nicci's and Nicci inched her lips closer to Pat's, there seemed to be only one inevitable conclusion.

'That was when we saw The Bear,' Pat told me. 'He was standing right in the middle of the kitchen floor, staring right at us. Dude, I'm telling you: it was like he was x-raying our souls. After that, the moment had gone. There was no way we could do anything. I'm glad, because we would have felt awful afterwards. I'm pretty sure that's the first time I've been cock-blocked by a cat.'

If any animal I'd known had shown a sign of having a moral compass, it was The Bear. He'd mysteriously vanished at some pretty important moments when he was young (house moves being chief among them), but as an older cat, he'd appeared equally inexplicably at just as many of them: moments when people were sad, or ill, or troubled. It wasn't as if he appeared in the way other cats do at these moments, strolling into the room in a way that said, 'Yep, I'm a cat, and I'm in your room because I go where I please.' It was more that he materialised, as might an enchanted vapour or a ghost from the future. I could imagine with little effort the situation Pat described.

In cat world, The Bear was a quiet, erudite observer, constantly learning and silently evaluating: the antithesis of the likes of Shipley, who bludgeoned their way to the centre of any social encounter, undeterred by how little of worth they had to say. It was a source of immense frustration not to be able to explain to all the cats why I was about to put them through another move – a bigger, more gruelling move than ever before – but when it came to The Bear, it was more than that. It was downright wrong. It felt as if you *should* be able to discuss important human matters with The Bear, because The Bear seemed so human. I could imagine him nodding thoughtfully as I told him: 'Norfolk is brilliant, and I have loads of great friends here, but it's a bit of a comfort zone for me. I want a fresh challenge, I want to be with Gemma and I get scared and a bit excited every time I think of Devon. I think it could be really good for you, too. A place where you could forget Biscuit. Not just forget her most hours, but draw a line under that whole episode and make a new start. The journey will be terrible but once you've done it, you'll never have to do it again, and you're going to be so much happier than you are here.'

The house we found to rent in Devon was the opposite of those I'd imagined: a two-hundred-year-old cottage made of traditional weathered granite, which wouldn't have been out of place in *The Hound of The Baskervilles*. Not resembling a 1960s doctor's surgery in the slightest, it sat high on a hill like the relish on top of the piled-up filling in a moor and sea sandwich: remote by rural East Anglian standards, but not, perhaps, by the more extreme and rugged ones of the rural South West. As an additional bonus, its kitchen had a hardwood floor, which meant I could slide the cats' food dishes to them across it and pretend they'd ordered whiskey off me in a saloon. If there were no hold-ups on the roads, we could probably complete the journey with all our stuff in no more than six hours.

Six hours: it wasn't really that much time, was it – the length of a flight from the UK to America's East Coast, or the sleep of a busy adult? I'd gone out last week into Norwich city centre, shopped at the supermarket and the hardware store, browsed in a couple of record shops and bookshops and met my friend Sam for a cup of tea, and that had taken six hours, and it had felt like no time at all.

This time there would be no overambitious attempts to save money by doing the move alone. A proper removal firm was booked, but even they underestimated slightly in terms of space. After they'd set off, the process of fitting our remaining stuff into the car and finding secure space for each of the four sumptuous new cat carriers I'd bought necessitated a last-minute jettisoning of several possessions. 'Let's face it,' Gemma and I reasoned to ourselves. 'Nobody really *needs* a toaster. Or coats.' A full container of cat biscuits was donated to the two kittens who lived next-door-but-one, but I left another small pile of them in the corner of the driveway for Gymcat, just to show there were no hard feelings. Actually, that's not true. There were lots of hard feelings, but he wouldn't have been able to read a note saying 'Goodbye Gymcat. *Try not to be a dick*', so I decided the best option was to try to mess with his head a bit.

Not before any house move in the past, not before any vet visit had I dreaded putting the cats in their carriers as much as I did as we began this journey. From a cat's perspective, good things rarely happen when you are put in a basket: you end up in scary new lands where other cats rule, or clinical white rooms where strangers stick needles in your neck or thermometers up your bottom. This, though, would be arguably even worse. 'We just need to get through the trip and we'll be OK,' became our mantra. If Gemma and I weren't saying it to each other out loud, we were repeating it in our heads. 'Wank sausage!' shouted Shipley as I coerced him into his plastic igloo. Ralph, who'd been looking particularly magnificent and Warren Beatty-like earlier that day, immediately began to meow his own name as soon as we got in the car, much as Warren Beatty probably would if you put him in a cage and drove him towards Dartmoor. Roscoe twisted very quickly onto her back, gazing up at the ceiling of her carrier as if struck by a terrible depression at finally having been forced to slow down and consider her place in society as a small black and white cat. The Bear's response to being placed in his carrier was the most painful of all to witness: a tiny, almost accepting *meeoop*, tinier than any *meeoop* he'd let out before, more plaintive than a plaintive song played by the world's tiniest violin. As I locked his carrier, I saw a tear roll down Gemma's cheek. We would not admit it until much later, but we were both thinking the same thing: would he actually make it through this?

Mercifully, there were no hold-ups on the journey. I'd like to say this made it bearable. In fact, even with that blessing it was a small version of hell. I'd done the same trip dozens of times over the last few years, yet the mere addition of four cats turned it into a quest, a heroic test of endurance that, when it was over, made you feel like one of life's survivors. Later, after arriving, Gemma and I would wonder if we had in fact died somewhere along the way and were now living in some kind of afterlife: very much like real life, but slower-moving and with much clearer air. 'No, that's just the West Country,' said Gemma's mum when we put this theory to her, but I couldn't be certain.

The first problem had been Ralph, who, after realising the tactic of meowing his own name wasn't working, spent much of the stretch between Reading and Bristol panting, yet refusing the water that Gemma, sitting beside him on the back seat, tried to give him. The Bear was amazingly, though also slightly worryingly, quiet, but Roscoe, still upside down, had clearly sunk into a deeper than ever depression. After a hundred-mile tirade of swear words, Shipley finally decided he'd had enough around the time we were passing Weston-super-Mare and, with one almighty shout of 'Bollock warehouse!', punched his way out of his carrier and onto my lap. Not particularly wanting to have a small, truculent animal stomping all over my crotch while I was in the fast lane of the M5 was one of my prime reasons for buying such large, solid carriers, but I'd underestimated Shipley, whose sheer force of will could have propelled him through the walls of San Quentin State Prison.

'Sure,' I thought, driving towards the next motorway exit for several miles with one hand on the wheel and the other on Shipley's scruff. 'Formula One drivers have a lot of skill, but the Monaco Grand Prix would be an entirely different prospect if they were each forced to complete it with a volatile black cat sitting next to them, repeatedly telling them to piss off.'

After we'd stopped and fastened Shipley back in, we never felt entirely confident it wouldn't happen again, and spent the remaining time in the car taking turns to hold the front of the igloo. This necessitated either me operating the car one-handed, or Gemma, who had severe backache, reaching over painfully from the back seat. To his credit, The Bear tried to create a more mellow atmosphere for everyone at this point by diffusing the aroma of a well-matured turd roughly half the size of his own body. This gave the leg of the journey between Taunton and Bovey Tracey a claustrophobic atmosphere that made us yearn for some of the trip's earlier parts in the way you might yearn for the freedom of a lost beautiful childhood summer. Around us in the car's footwells lay the scattered debris of our ordeal: electric cables, hats, loose CDs, an eruption of spilled crisps and crackers soggy with the water from the specially purchased bowls and pipettes we'd hoped the cats would drink from. We watched the road signs go by in the way you watch a clock in an exam room. We were just six individuals – all law-abiding, if you overlooked Shipley – moving from one rural English county to another. So why did it feel as if we were fugitives racing towards a border?

There's a moment when you drive into Devon from the east when something about the landscape changes decisively. It doesn't happen when you first cross from Somerset or Dorset, but about forty miles farther on. The hills begin to grow and hunch together more protectively, the greenness is that more vast and overwhelming and the rest of Britain begins to feel like another country. For me, this is more of a border than the one separating Devon from the ancient nation of Kernow, or even the imaginary cultural line that cuts the oft-neglected limb of Devon, Cornwall and west Somerset off from the remainder of the land mass. Now this border became more firmly established in my mind, as it marked the point where I realised we had successfully completed a cross-country house move. As we passed over it and, shortly afterwards, pulled off the dual carriageway, a calm descended on the car: the kind of calm that might descend after someone has unplugged a loud stereo playing a terrible song, or on diving off the busy deck of a boat into deep, tranquil water. For the next twenty minutes, until we arrived outside the house, nobody spoke. It was as if, knowing the finish line was within reach, we were using all of our concentration to focus on it. Outside the car, tall, insulating walls of green added to the silence. In the final ten minutes we passed just one other vehicle: a tractor.

A huge poetic moon hung over the cottage; a proper

country moon, taking advantage of the extra room it had to stretch out and be itself. When I turned the engine off, the car clock said midnight exactly, which would also have been poetic if my car clock wasn't always three minutes fast.

'We did it,' said Gemma.

'I can't believe it,' I said.

'Raaaallph,' said Ralph.

'Eat my furry fuck trousers!' said Shipley.

'Eweh,' said Roscoe.

'Meeoop,' said The Bear.

'Bloody hell. We live here,' I said.

'Big sex piss!' said Shipley.

Taking two cats apiece, we walked up the path to the front door. Behind us, out of the corner of my eye, I saw a dark four-legged form dart across the lane. A deer? Maybe. A fox? It was hard to tell. The moonlight was full of chicanery, making shapes appear larger than they were. My tired brain was untrustworthy, and I saw more shadow than anything, but after the thing crossed the road and entered the field to the left of the house, it appeared to curve back towards the rear of the building, as if it was not so much escaping from the human life it had chanced upon but circling it inquisitively.

# Cat Horoscopes

### Aries

This week you will see a ghost, but nobody will notice when you look startled about it, as you look like that a lot of the time anyway. Later, a serendipitous series of events – all vole related – will take you on a lengthy journey (247 yards). You will then wander back in your own sweet time.

### Taurus

Beware of not getting your rest. Less than eighteen hours of sleep can have a negative effect on your working life.

### Gemini

This week brings a significant fork in the road for you, in the form of having to decide whether to sit on two clean towels or in a plant.

## Cancer

Keep your friends close and your enemies closer. Unless your enemy is the vacuum cleaner or that powerful hairdryer Helen bought the other day.

## Leo

The time has come to make a change in your life. Primarily, stop following people to the toilet and sitting there staring at them. It's mega-creepy.

## Virgo

A tall dark stranger is set to walk into your life this week, and then walk out again, when you take a piss in his hydrangeas. However, do not fear, because soon after that wedding bells will ring! Not for you. You're a cat. But you'll hear them coming from a nearby church, and they'll annoy you.

## Libra

Your meow is actually really lame. Nobody has the guts to tell you normally, as they want to protect your feelings, but it's high time you knew the truth.

## Scorpio

The moment has come to ask some big questions, such as, 'If I puke on this sofa, does it officially count as mine?'

## Sagittarius

There is an ancient Eastern proverb that states: 'Something lost often leads to something found.' The coming few days will be a case in point, as you lose a collar but find some old toast to lick nearby.

## Capricorn

Go away. I am eating.

## Aquarius

This week you will ignore a toy your owner bought you but piss about for hours with the polystyrene packing beads it arrived with.

## Pisces

A big week for you! You'll lick a spider out of next door's tabby's ear and have a long, emotive dream about a beagle.

# I Put a Bell On You
# (Because You're Mine)

It was a cool spring night in the beer garden of The Torch pub, and the big topics were horses, cows and comic books. The first of these was providing the greatest entertainment value by a considerable distance. I was a little late to the party, but I'd just about picked up on the general gist of events. Earlier that week, a woman had been witnessed marching a horse up the extremely steep high street of the local town, Totnes, approaching pedestrians apparently at random and putting the question 'Would you like to buy my horse?' to them. This had caused quite a stir amongst residents, though perhaps not as big a stir as it might have done if it had happened elsewhere to Totnes: a town that had, until recently, made the claim on a road sign on its outskirts that it was 'Twinned With Narnia'.

'I don't think she managed to sell the horse in the end,' said Lee, one of my new Devon friends. 'But she gave it a

good go. I heard she tried the same thing in Buckfastleigh the next day.' He called over to a man on the adjacent table who resembled a cheerful nineteenth-century magician. 'Did she try to sell it to you, Bob?'

'No,' said Bob. 'But she tried to sell it to Eric from down Harberton way. He didn't want it. He's got an Irish Wolfhound and he's moving to Holsworthy, so he's got plenty on his plate already. I heard she even opened the door to the bakers and asked if anyone in there wanted to buy it. Nobody did.'

I'd only lived in the countryside surrounding Totnes for just over a fortnight, but already it felt at times like living in an unusually westerly Thomas Hardy novel, as reimagined by Timothy Leary. At the bottom of the valley, a steam train puttered along parallel to the River Dart, filling the air with the smoke and whistle of a gentle dream, while teenagers eschewed video games to paddle in the shallows or set off on kayak rides towards the coast. A permanent, pleasant smell of incense and woodsmoke lingered over the whole place, making you wonder if the huge industrial chimney near the train station was gently pumping out patchouli on a twenty-four-hour basis.

On a recent walk, I'd rounded a corner into town and within the space of no more than a minute had seen a child riding a unicycle, a woman wearing a burlap sack, a man taking a European eagle owl for a walk and a jogger clutching two marrows and a leek, with euphoria in his eyes. Boasting its own currency – the Totnes Pound, invented to support independent businesses – and with arguably more yoga instructors and organically farmed vegetables per square yard than any other market town in Britain, Totnes was its own self-contained world, but its eco-conscious, meditative outlook permeated the surrounding hills too, like a cloud of magic smoke.

Now, towards the top of one of those hills, in The Torch, the conversation turned from the horse to comic books, which Lee illustrated for a living and which two of Lee's friends, who were sitting beside us, read obsessively. I tried to keep up, but, not having read a comic book since I last opened a *Beano* annual on a family holiday during the mid-1980s, found myself flailing a bit.

'I'm terrible at drawing,' I said. 'I find cattle especially difficult.'

In truth, I couldn't remember ever trying to draw a cow and, if I had, certainly couldn't recall the level of difficulty involved, but I wanted to find a way of steering Lee in a bovine direction without appearing to commit too much of a non sequitur, and this was the best I could do. To be exact, I was looking for some advice on a group of twenty or so heifers in one of the nearby fields, who'd been giving me a fair bit of trouble recently. I'd already been venturing out with my Ordnance Survey map and doing lots of exploring in my new area, but all the most interesting routes involved passing these heifers, who would chase and crowd me every time I walked past them. I hoped that Lee, who'd grown up on a dairy farm, might be able offer some tips on the best way to pacify them.

'You say they're not very big?' he asked. 'If they're just young heifers, you probably don't need to worry about them. If they get bolshy, just wave your hands around a lot and shout "Whaaaaey".'

'Whey!' I said, giving it a practice run. I moved my arms around from side to side in front of me, in a fashion not dissimilar to the way somebody might during their favourite ballad at a concert by a large sentimental American rock band.

'Yep, that's it,' said Lee, kindly. 'But do it with a bit more enthusiasm and authority. Like, "Wwwwwhaaaa-eeeey!".'

Dave, The Torch's landlord, arrived at our table and scooped up a couple of empty pint glasses. 'Are you talking about cows?' he said. 'You want to watch out if you're walking through a field of them. My mate James Jameson has a farm up near Yelverton and he's had his foot broken four times by his Friesians.'

'Bloody hell!' I said. 'The same foot?'

'No,' said Dave. 'Different feet. Three times his left foot, once his right foot.'

Raising his eyebrows to make a 'Don't say I didn't warn you' face, he headed back towards The Torch's bar, with Snacks, The Torch's sandy-coloured resident cat, slinking along behind him.

The Torch wasn't actually called The Torch, but Gemma and I had got into the habit of calling it 'The Torch pub', since it was the only pub in the vicinity of our new cottage that you needed a torch to get back from safely at night. I learned this the hard way on my first walk there two weekends before the conversation about cows, during which I walked into a tree. Despite the resulting nose injury, I soon came to remember this as an idyllic first night out as a Devonshire resident, sound-tracked by the hoots of tawny owls and the purr of Snacks, who'd sat next to me for a large portion of the evening.

The Torch was only two or three football pitches' distance from our house, but, while not requiring the negotiation of any roads, reaching it necessitated fighting your way along a narrow path past fierce nettles and bracken. When we'd first met Snacks there a couple of months previously, after our first viewing of the cottage, we'd speculated as to whether we'd be getting any visits from him, and decided we'd probably be just beyond his territorial remit. We were proved wrong when, two days after we moved in, we found him in our back hedge, involved in a tense debate with Shipley over legal boundary issues.

Snacks was, according to local legend, a cat who got around a bit. 'He's a big problem, that one,' a carpenter who came to our house told me, going on to detail the time Snacks had been caught 'licking the cake' during a wedding at the big hotel on the other side of the village. Upon performing a couple of word searches relating to our new area on Instagram, one of the first things Gemma found was some photographs a couple of holidaymakers had taken during their stay in the rooms above The Torch, several of which depicted Snacks curled up happily on their bed, or drinking from the tap in their bathroom. Dave told me that an elderly lady in the village had woken in the middle of the night with a scream, noticing 'something moving under her duvet', only to find it was Snacks, who had let himself in through her bedroom window during the night. He had also been seen 'sitting in the front row before a couple of folk gigs at the village hall'.

Snacks was clearly none too happy with the arrival into his dominion of four feline invaders from the East, but his clashes with Shipley and Ralph didn't seem too heated. If there were some harsh words being exchanged and I went outside to intervene, Snacks always backed off instantly, seeming far more interested in the prospect of a cuddle with me than any aggro.

I'd not fully noticed it before we'd moved nearby, but

Totnes was a town that teemed with cats. It even boasted the UK's first cat café, an establishment where, for a small fee, cat lovers suffering from withdrawal symptoms for some reason or other could spend an hour or two drinking tea, eating cake and stroking one of six remarkably docile moggies. I assumed most of the café's clientele was tourist-based, as it was hard to imagine anyone who lived in Totnes suffering from cat withdrawal symptoms: you could barely walk the distance of three medieval cottages without another whiskery flirt emerging from a doorway or front garden and weaving his or her way around your ankles. Overspill left the surrounding countryside dealing with similar issues. I'd imagined that living a lengthy walk from town, in a house with no near neighbours, might create an interloper-free environment for The Bear, Roscoe, Ralph and Shipley, but we were already almost overrun with visitors. In addition to Snacks, these included a lanky ginger and white cat I'd seen a couple of times lurking in a bush beside our garden pond and a fluffy, lightning-fast grey cat who, in the words of our neighbour Amanda, was 'always going through people's cat flaps, doing a big shit in their living room, then leaving'.

While not exactly welcome, none of these foes appeared to present a source of anxiety for our cats on anything like the level Gymcat had. Roscoe, Ralph, Shipley and The Bear had already perked up noticeably since the move. On his first journey out of the garden, up onto a hillside meadow bursting with rabbits, blue-bells and primroses, I could have sworn I saw Shipley take a rare reflective moment to kneel, put his paws together and thank the great deity Ceiling Cat for delivering him to this place. The Bear, meanwhile, was spending more time outdoors than he had in three years – not venturing beyond the garden, but ecstatically sunning himself on the paving slabs by our new pond and watching the world keenly from the steps outside the back door. As I set off to explore my new area, OS map in hand, Ralph, Shipley and Roscoe would often follow me into the meadow, dictating that I had to turn back and find a way to give them the slip, for fear they would clash with those bolshy heifers.

Aided by Lee's advice, my own relationship with the heifers quickly improved: I began to stride boldly through them on my walks over the valley ridge towards the river. On early spring's first properly warm day, I'd begun a long walk in bare feet, stopping confidently among them, and one of them had strolled over and taken a couple of enthusiastic licks at my toes. I was trying not to let it go to my head or change me as a person but, if I was being totally honest, I was feeling pretty good about it.

For the second time in six months, by merely putting some possessions in a van and driving to a new home, we seemed to have moved the cats to an entirely new season. Spring always felt like an eruption in Norfolk, but a Norfolk spring is a small ornamental fountain in a garden pond by comparison to the psychedelic geyser found in Devon at the same time of year. Recent heavy rainfall, chased by a hot sun you felt as if you could reach up and touch, had rendered this part of the county virtually fluorescent. Looking down from the top of the hill over the adjacent valley to the cottage, bluebells could be seen marauding through the woods like a vast, galvanised blue army. Rambling along the narrow lane beyond the woods, I found a squirrel, recently dead, its paws covering its eyes as if it was just hiding from an especially scary bit in a squirrel horror film. The countryside surrounding the River Dart was all heartbreaking death on a tiny scale or exploding, widescreen life: one somehow impossible without the other. I woke up every day feeling lucky to live in such a vibrant, unspoilt landscape, but being that bit more untamed than rural Norfolk, rural Devon was also making me a little more aware that the countryside – especially when at its most wild and unspoilt – was streaked with blood.

Maybe it was sheer coincidence, but over a period of a month, nearly every person I met in Devon told me a tear-jerking story about a cherished animal in their life. A plumber who called over to stop the water in our taps being dark brown told me agonisingly of a strong gust of wind that had fatally blown his Jack Russell off a cliff near Teignmouth into the waves below. Having discovered I was an animal lover, our head removal man, Brian, had instructed me to ask his colleague, Clive, to tell me about the frog he befriended. 'He was just a frog I found one day, but he was lovely,' Clive said. 'I called him Fred. He used to sit on my shoulder and come to the shops with me.'

After several months of friendship, Clive arrived home from work one day to find Fred in the backyard, dead. 'A bird had got him,' he said, his voice catching in his throat. For the remaining hour spent unpacking the van, Clive remained very quiet and looked a little red around the eyes. Every few minutes, Brian made a small *ribbit* sound under his breath, and I regretted encouraging the telling of the story.

There's a line of thinking that claims people who've lived in the countryside for many years become hardened to the suffering of animals. This is not always true. I'd lived in rural places almost all my life, and I was probably more of a wuss than I'd ever been. There was a dead adder I'd seen two years ago, at the side of the A38, which I still thought about fairly regularly to this day. If I was driving along a country road and I saw a pheasant, I'd beep my horn at the pheasant, sometimes even if it wasn't on the road itself, in the hope that it might make it view roads as places where beeps happen and be more wary in future. I had not become immune to the sight of animal death or suffering – far from it – but I had become more accepting of it, certainly not as a sport, or by the hand of humans, but as a necessary by-product of the beauty of the countryside. It was possible to hide from it, but I'd tried that and it wasn't for me. I was an outdoor cat, and always had been.

It appeared, though, that, along with Ralph, Shipley, The Bear and Roscoe, I was becoming a bit more of an outdoor cat than ever before. You'd be insane not to, in a place like this, with so much going on. At my last

house I'd only *heard* foxes. Now I came face to face
with them on my walks along the riverbank at dusk.
Back in Norwich, the only thing in the chimney was a
load of old soot and, on his more troubled days, Ralph.
At the top of the one here there was a nest of jackdaws,
whose emo chirps echoed down and gave the living
room the atmosphere of a small abandoned vampire
church. At night, myriad animal noises could be heard:
some known, some unknown. Once, I was woken to
what sounded like a warthog slaughtering a guinea pig
behind the back hedge of the garden. Slightly fearful for
the cats' safety, I went outside and shone the torch in
the area where the sound had come from, but found
nothing. More often I'd be woken by the cries of tiny
beings being slaughtered by owls. Later, a screechy owl
would cry out and usually be answered by a calmer,
more concerned-sounding owl: a 'u ok hun?' of the
tawny universe. Gemma set her alarm early for work,
but it was superfluous. We already had Ralph's customary Ralph alarm – or the 'Ralarm' as I called it – and
the most energetic dawn chorus I'd ever heard to wake
us up every morning. Sometimes an owl who was burning the candle at both ends would even join in
incongruously with this, like Leonard Cohen walking
into a Shangri-Las recording session by mistake.

Arriving back home from a walk one day in mid-April,
I met the Easter Bunny. Actually, that's not true. I met a
third of the Easter Bunny. The other two thirds were
divided between the back porch and Shipley's stomach.
After their long winter layoff, an element of 'making up

for lost time' was noticeable in Ralph and Shipley's killing regime, and it was Devon's rabbits who were the primary victims. Even Roscoe, barely bigger than a rabbit herself, made an attempt to join in.

'Ah, don't worry about it,' a neighbour said to me, when I told him dolefully about the bloodshed. 'There's too many of them anyway. It's good. It keeps the population down.'

I felt bad for these rabbits, though. In a place that retained many 1960s counterculture ideals, they were the ultimate hippies: they didn't want to hurt anyone; all they wanted to do was eat their greens and have lots of unfaithful sex. Clearly nothing that they'd been put through by Snacks, Fluffy Grey Poo Burglar Cat, ginger and white Lurking Bush Cat or even the Needy Facebook Status Owl and its friend had prepared them for Ralph and Shipley's reign of terror. Caught in the melee was even a squirrel, which Gemma found upside down on the lawn, presumed dead, only for her to flip it over and watch it come back to life, urinate on her hands and escape into the hedge.

'OK, that's it!' I announced, after a particularly tough morning, featuring three rabbit casualties and a bout of strenuous carpet-cleaning. The next day, extra large bells, in addition to those already there, were affixed to Ralph and Shipley's collars. The kill count went down drastically after that, since making the sound of an approaching morris dance troupe is never going to be ideal when trying to creep up stealthily on your prey from behind.

In my initial fantasies about living in a low-density cat area, I'd hoped that this time we might be able to get by with a normal cheap cat flap, but, with the recent levels of leporid and rodent slaughter, and the worries presented by Fluffy Grey Poo Burglar Cat, I conceded, for the third house in a row, that a sturdy microchip cat flap was the only way to go. 'Tricky to drag a corpse through' wasn't explicitly stated in the marketing literature for the flap I chose, but I sensed it was implied. This new flap, I read, would store the microchip numbers of up to thirty-two cats. I couldn't help but be intrigued about the conversation that had led to this decision. I pictured two men with expensive haircuts sipping cappuccinos in a clean, minimalist room overlooking the east London skyline.

'So, Jago, going forward, how many cat numbers is this baby going to store?'

'I'm thinking, like, thirty-two.'

'OK, cool, man. I mean, owning thirty-two cats is fine, but thirty-three? Let's face it, that's just *weird*.'

Hearing the cats re-enter the house after their new Devon adventures, it only now fully occurred to me just how quiet they'd been in Norwich. Ralph and Shipley had always vocally celebrated their arrivals before that, and now the celebrations began again, more riotous than ever. It made you dwell on the origins of the term 'cat burglar'. I wasn't sure who'd first invented it, but presumably it wasn't someone whose cat shouted 'I'm fucking BACK' every time it came in. Even on the occasions when they hadn't caught a rabbit, a vole or a mouse, Ralph and Shipley still had plenty to report. Roscoe took her new kingdom far more in her stride, staying out for longer and arriving back in more nonchalant fashion. The Bear would spend many long minutes staring at the sensor on the cat flap in a way that seemed to say, 'I am not a number', but even he frequently came through his tiny door with a new, chirrupy sprightliness. He was more sociable than ever, appearing within a minute or two any time Gemma or I were in the garden, and more chatty than ever with it. The elongated *meeooop*ing he'd put into practice in Norwich while drinking from his bathroom water bowl had been tweaked and stream-lined into a symphonic early hours art form: his own, clean-living eulogy to the power of drink. He also had a new noise, which he often used to greet us, a sweet, almost fluttery high-pitched sound of the sort a giant bee who wanted to be your friend might make. When visitors arrived, he stuck around to say hello in a gre-garious manner that belied his introvert past, not even scarpering when my friend Rupert took his excitable four-year-old daughter Maebe upstairs up to the spare bedroom to say hello to him. 'He's got . . . eyes!' she remarked, and everyone agreed that she was correct. The Bear really did have eyes: soft, soulful ones that saw into you, eerily yet compassionately. In the clear Devon air, they seemed wider than ever.

Unlike Ralph, Shipley and Roscoe, it was not renewed bloodlust that had lifted The Bear's spirits since the move. A couple of times I'd found him

standing next to rabbits that Ralph and Shipley had left on the lawn, inspecting them, but his attitude suggested less that he was thinking about lunch and more that he was wondering if it was worth trying CPR on them. I still had no concrete evidence that he had killed another living creature in his entire eighteen and a half years on the planet. Looking out of the window of my study one day in May, however, I saw something genuinely shocking: a sight so contradictory to everything I'd learned about The Bear in the long time I'd known him that it literally caused me to rub my eyes and look again. As Ralph, Shipley and Roscoe watched from the lawn, The Bear, balancing on his hind legs, had the lanky ginger and white cat pinned against the garden's back fence. I rushed downstairs and through the back door, but, instead of taking immediate action, found myself pausing for a few seconds in admiration. It was not just that The Bear had faced down this significantly larger, vastly more youthful cat; he appeared to be doing what was essentially cat kung fu on him. Lunging forward, propelled by his back legs, in sharp bursts, he wheeled his front legs furiously and puffed his chest out, reminding me of angry desert lizards I'd seen on TV wildlife shows.

Was this really the same Bear who was now too arthritic to leap onto the kitchen work surface? Whose limbs folded beneath him slightly every time he made the sixteen-inch descent from his favourite chair to the living room floor? The cat who was so quiet and peace-loving that I suspected he secretly read my Penguin 20th Century Classics when I was not around? The ginger and white cat looked genuinely taken aback, and I did go over and call The Bear off after a short while, but I was flabbergasted and impressed. It was as if, after all the ferals who'd come and gone at the Upside Down House, after Gymcat and the ordeal of the subsequent move, a switch had clicked in The Bear's head and he'd said 'Right! No more! If nobody else is going to take a stand, then I will!' Was this in fact an intrinsic feature of The Bear that I'd never before recognised: that you could sick him on other people and animals you didn't like, in the way that anti-social owners of obedient yet aggressive dogs sometimes do? Excitedly, I began to make a mental list of people I abhorred. 'Bite his nose!' I imagined myself commanding, as The Bear advanced towards a quivering Jeremy Clarkson, or Nigel Farage.

He could certainly have picked a worthier target for his secret rage than the ginger and white cat. Gemma and I had got into the habit of calling this cat Darren, but it seemed less and less suited to him. Watching him toddle off sheepishly into the wild flower meadow behind the house, it occurred to me again how wrong I'd got him. I'd never seen Darren commit anything approaching an act of assault on any of my cats but, scarred by the Gymcat episode, I'd splashed water in his direction a few times on his early visits, taking him for another muscular thug who wanted the moon on a stick. Time had shown me his sweet nature and made me feel awful about that. He wouldn't let me near enough to touch him, though I'd managed to get a better look at him. His face had a few scratches, but it was a much kinder face than those of the ferals I'd known in the past, the face of a gentle cat who'd fallen on bad times rather than a hard-bitten survivor. I didn't have to inspect him very carefully to realise he still had his balls, since they were the size of two small, furry apples. Despite being bigger than all of my cats, apart from Ralph, he was younger than I'd initially presumed; certainly no more than two, maybe barely out of kittenhood. I asked around the village and in The Torch, but nobody had any knowledge of an owner, or anyone who'd lost a ginger and white cat answering to his description. Even after The Bear's kung fu attack, he continued to hang around, silently watching our cats from the undergrowth like a poor child from the orphanage spying on the privileged kids who had it all, wishing he could join in. At night, when it rained, he meowed dolefully below our bedroom window.

'Did you hear that?' I said, as Gemma and I listened to Darren.

'Hear what?' said Gemma.

'Geeeeeooooorrrge,' said Darren.

'That!' I said. 'It sounds like he's meowing the name "George".'

'I don't think it does at all,' said Gemma.

'Geeeeeooooorrrge,' said Darren.

'There it is again!' I said.

'Nope,' said Gemma. 'I think you're on your own here.'

'Geeeeeooooorrrge,' said Darren.

'Yep,' I said. 'Definitely George. We should call him George.'

'What if he ends up being our cat?' said Gemma. 'We can't have two cats who meow their own names. That would be stupid.'

'I suppose it would. But do you agree that it sounds more like he's meowing the name "George" than the name "Darren"?'

'Er, I suppose so, yes.'

'OK, that's settled then.'

'What's settled?'

'Nothing. Just . . . stuff.'

'Geeeeeooooorrrge,' said George.

It was now seven months since I'd sold the Upside Down House and said goodbye to its paranormal feral cat nest. I'd moved 350 miles, but apparently the curse had not lifted. The situation was the same: I had a stray russet-coloured cat in my garden, seemingly wanting me to look after it. Perhaps I was just a natural magnet for mangy gingers. 'Is this what it felt like to be an attractive female during the heyday of the band Simply Red?' I wondered. It was as if George had known we were coming here all along, and had been waiting for us in the undergrowth, right from that very first night. Or perhaps the shape I'd seen darting across the road under the giant moon had been him, timing his arrival perfectly to coincide with ours.

George was skinny, but not as skinny as many stray cats I'd seen. What had he been doing for sustenance? No doubt the bins behind The Torch had yielded a few tasty morsels and, what with Ralph and Shipley's recent activities, our lawn provided its own selection of offal canapés more days than not. I rarely had to clean up any vole or rabbit innards that Shipley or Ralph left on the grass because I could be certain they'd be gone within the hour. This tidying act could have been performed by George, but the more likely culprits were the jackdaws who lived at the top of our chimney. Their children were certainly not wanting for food, as I found out first-hand one morning when a remarkably plump one of them bumped down into our mercifully empty fireplace.

When the fledgling landed in the hearth I'd been

researching the history of Dartmoor and listening to a Nic Jones album. I'm not sure which of the two of us was more surprised: the jackdaw, about suddenly not being in a nest any more, and instead in a room smelling vaguely of nag champa listening to old folk songs about the devil, or me, about having a fat corvid in my fireplace – but I think he might just have edged it. Fortunately, all of the cats were asleep elsewhere in the house at the time. The fledgling and I stared at each other for a moment, then I walked over and picked him up. Appearing to be uninjured, he perched contentedly on my arm as I gave him a tour of the room in a way that suggested he'd done this sort of thing before, then sat placidly beside me while I telephoned a couple of bird rescue helplines.

I was told that my best course of action was to place the fledgling high up in a hedge, where he'd be away from ground-level predators and his parents would have the chance to see him. Watching carefully for any sign of George, I followed instructions and waited and watched for an hour, but the jackdaw just sat very still and no rescue team arrived from above. By this time, The Bear, Roscoe, Ralph and Shipley, who I'd locked inside the house, had got a whiff that I was up to no good behind their backs, and had gathered at the window to watch. This, I find, is one of the problems with time management as a self-employed writer living in the countryside with cats: you can block out time for work, but you rarely allow for the hour that you'll spend, say, looking for a dead vole in a wardrobe, or a member of the crow family whilst attempting to keep your cats, and the feral cat you're also trying to rescue, away from it.

I went back outside and picked the fledgling up again. It was raining hard out of a clear sky, and I had the hood up on my black anorak, adding to the scene's Hammer horror film quality. He seemed amazingly content to sit on my arm, had a lovely cheeky face and only smelt faintly of the devil's catacombs, but it clearly wasn't going to work between us. He wasn't going to get on with some of my friends, for starters. Another look towards the window, where some of them were currently gathered, went some way to confirming this.

In a last-ditch attempt to reunite him with his parents, I got a ladder out of the garage and climbed onto the lower part of the roof, but could not get within twelve

feet of where the nest was. I left him up there for a while, but he tumbled happily back to ground level and skipped back towards me. Leaving the cats locked in the house, I placed him on a lower ledge and went inside to call one of the wild bird rescuers I'd spoken to earlier who'd offered to take him in if the hedge plan didn't work. I was on the phone for no more than five minutes, but this was enough time, shockingly, for the fledgling to pass from life to death. I found him lying peacefully on the ground, on his side, beneath the ledge where I'd left him. The fall, surely, hadn't been what killed him, since it had been from just a few feet, and he'd part flown a far greater distance a few minutes earlier entirely unscathed. I could not believe that ginger George was the culprit, as I'd not seem him around that day, and for a stray cat to kill a bird and fail to eat it would defy all reasonable stray cat logic. Had the jackdaw been snatched, then dropped, by a sparrowhawk, perhaps, while I was inside? Could he simply have died of stress? He'd not seemed stressed, but how do you know for sure, with a jackdaw? It wasn't as if he was likely to have told me. It was a mystery. One thing was certain: I felt I had let him down, unforgivably.

Later that week, I received another piece of sad news – a few days earlier, Snacks had died of a heart attack. He was twelve: the same age as Shipley and Ralph, cats I did not view in any sense as 'old'. Tributes to him flooded in to Dave at The Torch from residents of the village, in addition to some from much, much further afield, and soon one wall of the pub became The Snacks Wall, displaying photos from those who'd crossed paths with him, many of them complete strangers to Dave. I'd not witnessed such a strongly felt tribute to a community cat since members of a golf club near one of my houses in Norfolk walked off the course as a mark of respect, mid-tournament, after hearing that Bob, the adopted club cat, had been run over.[1]

Here was Snacks getting inside the fridge in the kitchen in The Torch, and sitting in the middle of a bench of around a dozen people in the beer garden, nursing his own pint. There was Snacks in a stranger's car, and on another stranger's bed, looking equally at home in both scenarios. Snacks had been a cat more interested in the affairs of humans than those of other cats. He shared this characteristic with The Bear, but he expressed it in a different way: he was more tactile and exuberant; less discriminating. I'd expected him to be a small part of my life for a long time. I hoped that the recent addition of four cats of eclectic temperaments in his territory had not added to any discomfort he felt towards the end of his life, and I wished I'd got to know him better.

I'm sure I'd have begun to feed George anyway, but there is no doubt that the deaths of Snacks and the jackdaw influenced me to redouble my efforts to win

1 The tournament name was later changed to 'The Bob Cup'.

his trust. There'd been more than enough animal suffering for one spring, and Gemma and I were beginning
to realise exactly what a truly lovely cat George was. He
waited in the garden every morning, and every morning
after feeding Ralph, The Bear, Shipley and Roscoe, I
placed a bowl of food out for him, moving it a few
inches nearer the house each time. He always jumped
back nervously when I reached out to stroke him, but
within about three weeks, he would come within a foot
or so of me to eat, and within another week he was
eating from the dish as I held it. While not exactly over-
joyed at his presence, none of the other cats seemed
poised to file a written complaint on headed notepaper.
Shipley only got really sweary with him when George
got too close, and The Bear, in a typically understanding
and intuitive way, stopped the kung fu attacks. The final
move in my plan was a blatant piece of deception,
which a craftier cat might not have fallen for, but
George, who was turning out to be a simple soul, took
the bait. Spotting him in the garden, I left a full food
dish just inside the hall for him, with the front door
open. Then I waited three minutes for his inevitable
move, quietly slipped out the back door, shut it, then
went around and shut the front door behind him, block-
ing the cat flap from the outside.

The transformation was instant. The second I picked
him up, all the feral anxiety seemed to drain out of him.
Within five minutes he was on my lap, purring: a long
strip of glad, furry warmth. His tomcat fragrance was the
only unpleasant thing about him. This was a cat whose

face radiated peace and love. He felt and acted so differently to the ferals I'd come close to before that that
afternoon I made some more enquiries among my neighbours. Were they sure they didn't know anyone who'd
lost a cat answering to his description? I also posted
photos of him on Twitter and Facebook, wondering if a
heartbroken owner might come forward. Surely George
had once known love? He appeared too soft, too
instantly mellow and trusting, to have lived a predomi-
nantly wild life.

What on earth had happened, to bring him here? I
began to concoct stories about him: a heartbreaking
escape from a car in a service station car park, a distraught
family, a long, lonely trek through alien countryside; an
unfortunate sleep in an ill-chosen box, a van loaded late at
night, a rude, terrifying awakening in a new environment.
Not since The Bear's six-week disappearing act in south
London in 2001 had I been keener for an animal to tell
me what it had been up to.

There was, of course, another possibility: that George
was simply a cruelly abandoned cat who'd been born
with an unusual, special kind of pliable good nature.
The following day, our vet checked him for a microchip
identification and found nothing, adding that she
couldn't remember encountering a feral cat of such
mellow and cooperative temperament. As a compliant
George sat on her examining table, I faced a familiar
choice: pay to have him inoculated, neutered, cleaned
up, tested for feline AIDS, then take him home; or leave
him there, allow the RSPCA to take care of him and

never see him again. Gemma and I took the evening to think and talk it over, but there was always only one decision to be made. We'd agreed that four cats represented catpacity for us, but could that be overruled, when a cat had come to find *us*? Was five *really* all that many? We had more than five moths living in our house, and nobody thought that was weird. I suspected George could be very good for our equilibrium, too, like having a really nice hippie friend around the house. I felt calmer just looking at his face, in the same way that I felt calmer when I stared at a sunset or listened to David Crosby's first solo LP.

The following day I picked up an arguably even mellower George from the vet. The last time I'd paid to have a cat's balls cut off that cat had subsequently, quite understandably, run away for ever, but George responded in amazingly sanguine fashion, which was perhaps even more impressive, considering the size of what he'd lost. He sauntered quite coolly around the house and raised no complaint when I rested matching flower-power daisies in our hair and took a photo to mark the occasion. Later, I read for a while on the bed and he appeared a little nervously at the doorway then jumped up and made his first foray onto the duvet, testing its surface excitedly. He looked slightly disbelieving, as if he was wondering if somebody was playing an elaborate joke on him, and would never have imagined in his wildest dreams that something so soft, dry and warm could exist.

Gemma, thinking back anxiously to the episode with Graham a couple of years earlier, suggested that perhaps we should keep him inside for another week, but I had an instinct that George would be fine returning to the outdoors. Sure enough, when I let him out two nights after his operation, his calmer indoor persona remained. There was no attempt to run or hide. Why would there be? He'd landed on his feet, and he knew it. We're told that cats always land on their feet, so that part was no surprise. What was a surprise was the speed of the landing. A week later, he was following me up into the meadow beside the house, with Ralph and Shipley bringing up the rear, on a daily basis. The cows were gone now. Wild flowers bloomed all around us. He gazed beatifically as butterflies flitted in rings above him. It was a scene he looked utterly at home in – more at home, perhaps, than I'd ever seen a cat before. He would hurtle ahead of me and shoot up trees, then I'd get ahead of him and he'd catch me up, cutting in front of me and standing proudly at my feet, almost doglike, his strong tail thwacking against my legs. 'I own you,' his body language seemed to say. 'In fact, I'll dispense with the modesty and be honest: I own this entire land, as far as the eye can see.'

# Advice for New Owners of a Formerly Homeless Cat

## Getting Your Homeless Cat Accustomed to His New Environment

The first week or two with a homeless cat are always the hardest. Despite having food and shelter, your homeless cat might crave the struggling life he came from, purely out of habit. This is completely normal. Look for little signs, such as your homeless cat stealing cigarettes or sitting inside old cheap bags near the exit of your garden.

## Signs that Your Homeless Cat Is Putting on a False Front For Your Benefit

Once settled into your household, your homeless cat might pretend to relax, just because he doesn't want to worry you and is keen to fit in. Remember: he might look loose and floppy but is probably deeply stressed underneath and turning the world's problems over in his anxious mind.

## Your Homeless Cat and the Internet

Homeless cats almost never have access to the Internet. To boost your homeless cat's self-esteem and make him feel part of the modern world, make a web page for him. Here, for example, is my homeless cat looking pleased after I have helped him start his own lifestyle and fashion blog.

## Teaching Your Homeless Cat About Nature

Psychologically, being a homeless cat can be incredibly traumatic. A good way to help your homeless cat get over this is to have a 'nature day' together. Head to the nearest nice countryside near your house and walk your homeless cat unhurriedly around it, being careful to notice the beauty of the landscape and simple, wonderful things, such as flowers and butterflies.

## Comforting Your Homeless Cat at Bedtime

If your homeless cat is sleeping with his paws over his eyes, this probably means he is dreaming about bad things, such as being chased by a badger, having to break into an out-of-service bus to find somewhere to sleep, or the prospect of five more years of a Conservative government. If so, try not to wake him, but gently place a blanket over him to offer him some comfort in his night-time torment.

## Your Homeless Cat and Music

Most domesticated cats like complicated jazz or edgy music made in urban areas, but homeless cats tend to prefer the more bucolic, dropout music of the 1960s counterculture, which speaks to them more directly. Play lots of this music to your homeless cat. This will make your homeless cat feel simultaneously more at home and more himself.

## The Surprising Sophisticated Side of Homeless Cats

It might be tempting to offer your homeless cat very basic drinks at first, such as Special Brew, Kestrel lager or some old rainwater that has pooled outside the house in a disused bin lid. Many homeless cats will feel deeply patronised by this, and actually far prefer the chance to indulge in a sophisticated glass of Pinot Grigio or filtered tap water.

## Steering Your Homeless Cat towards a More Mindful Life

Meditation is a great way to calm your homeless cat's mind. Many cities and small towns run meditation classes nowadays, especially if you live in the South West of England. Alternatively, light a candle, put on some soothing whale music and encourage your cat to meditate at home. If all goes to plan, soon he will have stopped dwelling on thoughts of his troubled past and uncertain future and be ready to live happily in the present, with you.

# The Summer of Love

Our public line on the George situation, for the time being, was that we were 'just fostering him'. At some point we would find him another nice home, perhaps with fewer cats to contend with, but until then, we were happy for him to live with us. Especially happy, in my case. 'You don't want a really brilliant ginger cat, by any chance?' I'd ask people. But I noticed that I had a habit of directing the question at the least likely takers: a friend's elderly mum, for example, who was poised to spend three months on an around-the-world cruise, or a gruff mechanic who mended my car and had earlier told me, with what I thought I detected was a bit of pride, that he was chronically allergic to all pets. For all my genuine intent, I might as well have asked the Francis Drake statue in Plymouth city centre, too. Meanwhile my bond with George swiftly grew and solidified. I had found out, for example, that as well as being very good to have around the house as a cat, he made an equally useful scarf, hat, pillow and blanket, his multipurpose nature made all the more pleasant by the fact that his pungent man fumes were dissipating with each passing day. He was not, in any sense, a complainer. Like Ralph, a growl was not part of his vocabulary. His dialogue was mostly limited to saying 'Geeeeoorge' and greeting me every morning with a friendly wibble at the bottom of the stairs.

The 'fostering' stance was, above all, a useful decoy when talking to my parents. Both of them could worry for England in midfield, wowing crowds with their creative interplay, and few of their worries were bigger than their long-time concern that I would render myself homeless and destitute by opening a multistorey hostel for down-and-out cats.

'Oh, *Tom*,' my mum said, in a despairing tone, when I told her about George.

'WHAT HAS HE DONE?' I heard my dad say in the background.

'He's only gone and got another cat,' said my mum.

'ANOTHER ONE?' said my dad. 'DO YOU THINK HE MIGHT BE GAY? TELL HIM THAT IF HE'S GAY HE CAN TELL US. WE'RE COMPLETELY OK WITH IT. HE DOESN'T NEED TO BE WORRIED.'

'I can hear everything you're both saying, you know,' I said.

'Raaaaaallllph!' said Ralph.

'You're not going to keep him, are you?' asked my mum. 'Just tell us you're not going to keep him. It will make your life a lot more difficult.'

'It's a cat we're talking about, not an unwanted teenage pregnancy,' I said. 'Anyway, he mostly lives outside. We'll find him another home eventually, but he's fine here for now.'

There was, however, the welfare of the other cats to think about. Shipley, The Bear, Roscoe and Ralph might have been relatively relaxed about sharing a garden with George, but whether they were equally acquiescent about sharing food bowls, sofas and newly washed jumpers with him was another matter entirely. 'Watch out! He's got a gun!' one of them would often shout during George's early days living with us, as he ambled innocently towards them. Hearing this, George would simply flop down on his side and reply, 'Look at the clouds in the sky, guys. Some of them look like sheep. Isn't our planet a beautiful thing?' They had got him very wrong. He was in it only for the love: a fact that had been amply illustrated during one of his first trips outside as a kept cat when he purred at a bee. The one time he had come anything like close to retaliating to one of Shipley's swearing sessions was when he had arched his head at an odd angle to him while walking away and making a noise resembling those of the children's TV characters, Bill and Ben The Flowerpot Men. In the end, though, you had to look at the facts: he was a strong, young, large and, until recently, sexually intact male cat, and Shipley, Ralph and The Bear weren't. This didn't seem to bother The Bear, who exempted himself from the tawdry business of masculine sparring, but, for Roscoe and Shipley, George was essentially a walking, purring sign which read: *Neither of You are As Young As You Used to Be.*

It was Roscoe, though, who was most troubled by

George's presence. Something had happened between George and Roscoe, not long before I first lured him into the house. Gemma and I weren't sure about the exact details but there'd been a loud noise and Roscoe had burst through the cat flap, showing liquid evidence of the scuffle on her fur. 'Has that cat got semen on its back?' was not a sentence I'd had call to use before and I hoped it wasn't one I'd have to use again. We hadn't panicked about it especially, reasoning that if George did think of Roscoe in that way, he'd begin to think of her in a different way once he was no longer chained to the idiot that was his libido. Also, back when he'd been living in the garden, I'd seen Roscoe sitting companionably alongside him under his favourite bush a few times. But now every time he saw her he bounded excitedly after her, as if he was Lennie from *Of Mice and Men* and she was a particularly soft rabbit. Along with his forays up trees on our walks together, this was one of the few occasions when there was any real urgency about George. His natural condition was to remain as horizontal and meditative as possible. Or perhaps he just had an unusual amount of cosy sleep to catch up on after his long winter fending for himself outdoors.

'HAVE YOU DRUGGED THAT CAT?' asked my dad, on seeing George, passed out on my lap, for the first time.

'No, he's nearly always like this,' I said, draping George around my neck. 'You can do this with him too. He doesn't mind.'

'HE LOOKS STONED OFF HIS FACE.'

I placed George, who still hadn't fully woken up, back on my lap. 'You can have him if you want.'

'NO. I'LL LEAVE IT, THANKS. FLOYD IS KILLING FOUR MICE A NIGHT AT THE MOMENT. HE GOT RODENT BLOOD ALL OVER ONE OF YOUR MUM'S LINOCUT PRINTS, AND CASPER HAS BEEN IN A LOT. HE'S STARTED HUMPING TOILET ROLLS. WE HAVE TO BUY EXTRA FROM ASDA NOW. SO WE'VE GOT ENOUGH GOING ON AS IT IS.' He rushed to the window. "BILL KINNELL! IS THAT A WOODPECKER?"

It was my parents' first trip to see me in Devon, and the countryside around Totnes had put my dad in what was, even by his standards, an excitable mood. One reason I knew this, is that when he'd seen the woodpecker in my garden, he'd shouted 'BILL KINNELL!' instead of just 'FOOKIN' 'ELL!' as he normally might have. Bill Kinnell was a man with one hand who ran a jazz club in Nottingham in the 1960s and whose name soon became a popular expletive among its denizens. My dad still used it even now, but tended to reserve it for occasions when he was particularly alarmed or enthusiastic. On our walk earlier that day, upon spotting the steam train chugging towards us alongside the River Dart, he'd shouted, 'BILL KINNELL!' then ran parallel to the train, cheering, for several hundred yards. Gemma, my mum and I caught him up ten minutes later, standing beside the river admiring the clarity of the water.

'I TELL YOU WHAT, IF MALCOLM WAS HERE HE'D STRIP NAKED AND JUMP RIGHT IN THAT,

NO MESSING,' he said. 'YOU LIVE IN THE BLOOMIN' 1950s HERE. I WISH I LIVED IN THE 1950s.'

'But you did live in the 1950s,' I said.

'YEAH, BUT IT WAS A DIFFERENT ONE. IT HAD LUNCHEON MEAT AND SMOG.'

We passed through a gate and crossed the train track. 'DON'T STEP ON THAT RAIL OR YOU'LL GET ELECTROCUTED.'

The following morning, Gemma and I both had to work, so my parents had planned a trip to the beach. By the time I was up, at just gone seven, my dad was already dressed, packed and ready to go. I found him outside in the chilly post-dawn air, sunning himself, topless, on a deckchair. Directly across from him, on a wooden table, sat The Bear, appraising his naked torso with some interest.

'HE KEEPS STARING AT ME,' said my dad. 'LOOK AT HIS FACE. I CAN'T BELIEVE HIS FACE. I DON'T KNOW WHAT HE WANTS. HE LOOKS BETTER THAN HE LOOKED A WHILE AGO. IT MUST BE THE AIR. I'VE MADE SOME COFFEE. I MADE IT THE WAY GEMMA LIKES IT, NOT THE WAY YOU LIKE IT.'

'Is your dad not cold?' Gemma asked when I returned to the kitchen.

'I don't think so,' I said. 'It's weird: he only seems to feel the cold when he's inside. He always has the car heater cranked up to the maximum, even in summer, and the fire on at home, but my mum found him sleeping outside with just a T-shirt and his boxer shorts on back in January.'

'Did you know he's got a snake in the glove compartment of his car?'

'No, I didn't. But it doesn't surprise me. I'm hoping it's not alive?'

She took a sip of coffee, winced and placed the almost full cup in the sink. 'I don't think so. Actually, now you mention it, I didn't ask. I just heard him talking to your mum about it.'

'Is it true you've got a snake in the glove compartment of your car?' I asked my dad later, when he and my mum got back from the beach.

'NO. IT'S IN THE OVERHEAD POCKET WHERE I NORMALLY KEEP MY SUNGLASSES. DON'T WORRY. IT'S DEAD.'

'What kind of snake is it?'

'IT'S JUST A NORMAL GRASS SNAKE, I THINK. IT'S QUITE SHRIVELLED NOW. I FOUND IT A COUPLE OF WEEKS AGO ON THE FOOTPATH WHEN I WAS WALKING NEAR CASTLE RISING IN NORFOLK. I WENT TO A POSH ART GALLERY AFTERWARDS. I WALKED AROUND A BIT AND FORGOT I WAS HOLDING IT. I GOT SOME RIGHT FUNNY LOOKS.'

'Ow!' I said.

'OOPS. SORRY. I FORGOT ABOUT YOUR SCAR. I WAS DOING THAT BECAUSE THAT'S WHAT I SOMETIMES DO TO MALCOLM. HE LIKES IT WHEN I DO IT QUITE HARD.'

As he told me about the snake, my dad had been standing behind the chair I was sitting in, roughly massaging my head. In a somewhat gung-ho move across my scalp, he'd caught the scab on the still fresh wound where, until five days previously, a large benign cyst had been growing. This was one of two cysts the household had been required to seek medical attention for recently, the other being located on The Bear's back. 'I think it's just a trapped hair follicle, but I'd better check it out,' The Bear's new Irish vet had told me before disappearing, with The Bear, into the bowels of his surgery. Three minutes later they arrived back in the main examination room. 'This is going to sound very weird,' he said, 'but it seems to have vanished. Have a look yourself if you like.' I examined The Bear's back and the skin was indeed now completely smooth and flat. In the month since then, the cyst had not reappeared, which was more than I could say for my own lump, which had gone under the knife twice to date and which I could already feel regrowing for a third time. Had my doctor not been so nice, I might have been tempted to go back to the vet's on my own and ask him if he could take me into his back room and attend to me too.

All this was typical of The Bear's uncanny resilience and our contrasting fortunes, since moving to Devon. In three months, The Bear had got ever shinier, more athletic, hungrier, more outdoorsy. My own health pattern was somewhat more chequered. I could see the fresh South West air having a positive effect on my skin and hair, and I was springy and nimble from the hundreds of miles I'd already walked here along riverbanks, up tors and over moors. But since arriving in Devon, I'd suffered a succession of ailments that I might have considered myself unlucky to pick up in the space of a whole year in gentle Norfolk. There was the spider bite I received, for example, when weeding the garden pond, which caused my forearm to swell to one and a half times its usual size; and the two greedy, fat-bottomed ticks I'd found feasting on my torso after a long walk around one of the remotest parts of Dartmoor. Then there were the several dozen stings I suffered on the first truly hot day of the year when, clad only in swimming trunks, I fell into a bed of nettles while saving a rabbit from Shipley. Worst of all was the urinary tract infection I'd sustained, which left me weeing blood and walking around dizzily with a high fever and chest pains, not fully knowing who or where I was.

What had caused this infection? The river swimming I'd been doing? One of those ticks? Neither I nor my doctor could be sure. One thing was for certain: there was a far wilder and more dangerous aspect to Devon's countryside than that of Norfolk, where the most I'd worried about on a walk had been whether I'd be trampled by cows or shot by a farmer who didn't like hippies. Even the beetles were bigger and bolshier here. One that had recently sauntered into our bedroom was so large and colourful it seemed to demand its own theme tune. Not that I wanted to shut my windows to any of this, or hide from it. I just hadn't quite expected it, what with the fact that I'd moved fairly near to Torquay, not Borneo.

In my below-par state, the cat I could find most

solidarity with was Ralph. Always a magnet for parasites, he'd been set upon by several of Devon's thirstiest ticks in the warmer weather. He'd also received a bite on his leg, which had turned into a large abscess, causing him to limp around very forlornly. The perpetrator of the bite remained a mystery, since George and Ralph seemed to be adopting a 'live and let live' policy around each other, and nobody had seen Fluffy Grey Poo Burglar Cat for many weeks. The ensuing journey to the vet's was a traumatic one for Ralph, who, remembering his last car trip, probably had terrifying visions of a six-hour drive back to see Gymcat. On the way, I attempted to soothe his *raaaalph*ing by listening to his concerns carefully and responding to them with as much thought and insight as I could.

'Raaaaallllph!' said Ralph.

'Don't worry,' I said. 'It won't be long. It's only ten or so minutes' drive. It will be over before you know it, I promise.'

'Raaaaallllph!'

'No, there are absolutely no motorways. Just country lanes and B roads.'

'Raaaaallllph!'

'No, I can't promise there won't be a Jack Russell there, like last time. If there is, just ignore it. The only reason they bark is because they have sad, lonely lives and want attention.'

'Raaaaallllph!'

'You're right. Kurt Russell's hair *was* great in John Carpenter's 1982 remake of *The Thing*. And you *could* probably get yours to look like that too if you wanted.'

'Raaaaallllph!'

'No, you'd barely have to do anything to it at all. You're pretty much already there.'

'Raaaaallllph!'

'It's true: you probably do have fluffier toes than him.'

'Raaaaallllph!'

'You want to listen to the third Led Zeppelin album? Seems a strange time for it, but OK – if you insist.'

'Raaaaallllph!'

Once we'd arrived at the vet surgery, he became his trusting self again. He was amazingly calm as the vet and I held him and the vet lanced his wound, releasing a quantity of yellow pus that would easily have filled a small ice cream cone. Perhaps more impressively, he also retained his equilibrium prior to that, while we sat in the

waiting room for three-quarters of an hour next to a noisy goose called Bob who had a poorly eye. Back at home, I cracked open a can of tuna for him and it was as if the whole episode had never happened.

Ralph and I had always had a fair bit in common. We were both quite hairy, and I liked to think we enjoyed the same records. He was the cat who most often sat next to me on my desk while I worked, often moving to my chair itself if I made the mistake of leaving the room for twenty seconds. I'd not really been able to empathise with his parasite problems in the past, but now we had that to bond over, too. I even had my own sympathy bite to go with his, which, though not escalating into an abscess or causing me to limp, had been fairly painful at the time and left large purple teeth marks on my left thigh. This was the methodical work of a German short-haired Pointer who'd burst out of a drive on a steep, quiet lane outside Totnes on one of my long country walks. It had all happened very quickly and systematically, as if the Pointer had been planning it for weeks. If a middle-aged man with an Oxbridge voice hadn't shouted 'Poppy!' just at the precise moment it began to sink its teeth into me, the wound would probably have been a lot worse. As I walked briskly away, I wondered what could possibly have prompted the man to give the dog such a name. Even ignoring the fact that it had attempted to maul me, it was one of the most un-Poppyish dogs I'd ever seen. If he'd shouted 'Lizzie' or 'Miley' or 'Gargantuan Cock Wand' at it, everything would have made sense, but not 'Poppy'.

A few miles farther into my walk, I would wish I'd

stopped and had stern words with the man, but I think it was only then, as my thigh began to throb, that the full realisation dawned on me that I had in fact sustained my first ever dog bite, rather than just been kissed by a dog with reckless and unwelcome intimacy.

Just twenty minutes prior to the bite, I'd been striding along the riverside path in the sun, past cheerful Labrador walkers, thinking about what a great place this would be to walk a dog. I'd enjoyed borrowing friends' and neighbours' dogs to walk in the past and, while I had no intention of inflicting a waggy-tailed idiot on the cats on a full-time basis, I fancied giving it another go. If I was a more superstitious person, I might have seen the Pointer's attack as a negative sign. Instead, I decided to reject fate's plan for me and mess with destiny's head by ramping up my search for a part-time dog. The following day, for the very reasonable sum of one pound, I placed an advert offering my services in the village post office on a wall densely populated with flyers for men and their vans, yoga retreats, second-hand fridges and evening talks on sacred geometry.

```
NEED YOUR DOG WALKING?

I am looking for a dog to take on long walks
around the South Hams countryside and beyond,
preferably on Wednesday or Thursday afternoons.
I have lots of experience walking friends' dogs
and especially like Spaniels, Border Collies
and any dog with a fringe that makes them look
slightly like a shoegazing musician from the
early 1990s. Please call Tom on ████████████
```

After a week, the ad had drawn a blank in terms of responses, and I'd got little further in my other attempts to find a dog to borrow in the area. I could borrow a Terrier belonging to a friend of a friend, but he was only available on Wednesdays, needed to wear a muzzle if he was being walked in an area where there were lots of other dogs and would reportedly attack any cat he saw. Gemma's mum's dog, Scrumpy, was also not greatly sociable when outdoors, and was liable to punch me. A Labrador belonging to a hairdresser in Exeter was available for walks, but when I had been to get my hair cut there and said, 'Please can you take hardly anything off at all?', she'd misheard me and thought I'd said, 'Attack my hair like it's a hedge in a sunny period in June immediately following heavy rainfall.' Would borrowing her dog mean a long-term commitment to looking like I worked in an insurance broker's office in 1949? I worried.

In desperation, I touted my dog-walking services on Twitter. There were still no local takers, but a couple of my followers recommended a dog-walking site called borrowmydoggy.com, which, for a very reasonable subscription fee, aimed to connect dog owners who needed minders for their dogs with enthusiastic dog borrowers, putting them in mutually beneficial, committed long-term relationships.

On signing up to borrowmydoggy.com, I felt both excited and overwhelmed. Here was a large array of eager-looking dogs, all within a ten-mile radius of my home, all just a simple message away. I immediately began to make a shortlist. High up on it were Rico and Raffi, two sibling

Lagotto Romagnolos, described as 'boisterous' and 'gentle-natured' – both of whom looked like they could easily have been fronting a 1970s stoner rock band. I also had my eye on Max, a Splurcher with a slight problem in the area of 'licking food', and Indie, a cheeky Spoodle who appealed to me in no small part because of her resemblance to the children's book character What-a-Mess. Unlike Gemma, who is the kind of person who will see a stranger's Rottweiler and run straight up to it and kiss it on the cheek like it's a favourite uncle, I felt a bit warier around big dogs. This was perhaps partly due to my dad's habit of shouting, 'WATCH OUT FOR THAT – IT WILL HAVE YOUR FACE OFF' every time I went for a walk with him and we saw one, but now Poppy had a bit to answer for, too. The bruise on my thigh had faded, but still stung each time I got in the bath or put on my jeans. I decided the upper size cut-off point in my dog-borrowing criteria was somewhere in the region of Border Collie. My lower size cut-off point wasn't too rigid, but I decided I would prefer not to walk a dog I could mistakenly step on, or who was liable to be seriously challenged in a fight with a rowdy duck. I also wanted a dog who preferably got on with cats, had no problem with long walks, had hair not unlike Keith Richards did in 1969 and wasn't called Poppy. I realised that dog-borrowing was already doing for me what online dating does for many others: it was turning me into a box-ticker, making me realise I had a 'type' when previously I'd considered myself open-minded.

Another similarity between dog-borrowing and online

dating is that it fosters a vacillation between egotism and anxiety. The first impression is that you are looking at a whole train carriage's worth of dogs, all of which are potentially available to you. The gradual realisation follows that there are many other people also competing for the train carriage full of dogs, a number of whom are potentially more qualified than you for dog-borrowing. It is important not to get your heart too set on a dog early on, or build that dog up too much in your mind, but both things are easier said than done. I 'favourited' Max the Splurcher once, then unfavourited him and favourited him again, in a somewhat undignified bid to get his attention, but, after two weeks, he still hadn't got in touch. After no reply from Bentley, a young Cockapoo, I found myself re-examining my profile picture, taken in 2011, in which I was wearing a synthetic fur trapper's hat I got cheap off Norwich market and crouching in a field in Norfolk with my friend Hannah's Cocker Spaniel, Henry. Perhaps it would be best if I lost the hat, I wondered. Had my appearance changed too much in three years? Maybe I needed a more up-to-date, honest photo? There was also no reply from Indie, the mini What-a-Mess dog, to my opening message, and I wondered if I'd come on a bit strong, suggesting a first walk straight away – or as BorrowMyDoggy call it, a 'Welcome Woof' – before we'd even got to know a few basic details about each other.

After a fortnight on borrowmydoggy.com, I'd set up three Welcome Woofs: one with an elderly Bichon Frise called Bess who lived a few miles away on the coast; one with Billy, a toy/miniature Poodle cross who lived on the edge of Dartmoor; and another with a family of four Spaniels just down the road from me. My mysterious river infection, which had faded a bit with my third course of antibiotics, came back with a vengeance on the day I met the Spaniels, Charley, Emily, Holly and Coco, and our Welcome Woof turned out to be more like an introductory dog riot. Walking four dogs, it transpires, is far more difficult than walking one, especially when it involves medieval, narrow-pavemented Devonshire streets and the South Coast traffic of a hot summer. By the end, even with Gemma there to take a couple of the leads, I was a sweaty mess, my T-shirt covered in lint, river mud and unidentified dog paste, and six turds in bags in my pocket, cooking in the midday sun. My walk with Bess a few days later, on the other hand, was a little too sedate: being eleven years old, she was unable to walk much farther than a mile.

Billy, however, was a delight: small, shaggy and relentlessly energetic, a small man in a dog suit, doing all the correct dog things. I'd not had any particular fondness for Poodles in the past, but he wasn't one of those Poodles you sometimes get who are constantly worrying about their hair and get uppity if you don't compliment them on their appearance every six minutes. He had no problem with getting a bit muddy and gave the impression, beneath his woolly exterior, of being made out of strong elastic. His owner, an occupational therapist called Susie, and I hit it off straight away and, after our first walk, we took him back to meet the cats. Roscoe, Ralph and George weren't around but, as was often the case nowadays, The Bear and Shipley immediately came out to say hello. The Bear kept his distance from Billy, eyeing him with ironic disdain from a garden chair, but Shipley strolled over, and a canine–feline stand-off followed. Small black dog and wiry black cat each feinted a few times, like footballers playing mind games with one another, until Billy sprang forward, chasing Shipley into a bush. Susie and Gemma and I raced after them, but before we could reach the bush there was a violent rustle of leaves, a loud scuffling sound and a couple of violent expletives, and a moment later, with an almighty whimper, Billy twanged out of the bush backwards, as if propelled by a catapult. Shipley followed about twenty seconds later at a more sedate pace, then rolled over on his back on the front step, stretching one casual paw out in front of him. As opening encounters go, it could have been worse, but I resolved to keep Billy apart from the cats as much as possible in the future – perhaps as much for his sake as for theirs.

I still felt weakened by my infection, suffered from chest pains and winced with rusty dagger pain every time I urinated, but I was determined not to let it stop me going out and enjoying the summer in this endlessly green new place I felt so fortunate to live in. The mere idea of not being outdoors when the sun shone here felt like slapping some benevolent pagan god in the face. Every Tuesday in June and July Billy and I walked until we – OK, until I – couldn't walk any more, stopping to swim in rivers and the clear sea just off what I didn't realise at first was my closest nudist beach. It was at the latter location that I faced my first big challenge as an Internet dog borrower. As I swam in the warm water, enjoying the rays of a sun that felt as if it was only a few hundred yards above me, I noticed that Billy, back on the shore, was taking a great deal of interest in the more delicate part of a naked hippie's anatomy. I weighed up the situation and decided I was faced with two options: charge out of the sea and remove him from the area in question, or shout, 'Hey! Leave that man's genitals alone!' in my new, commanding Dog Walker's Voice. Having given both options some serious consideration, I decided instead to pretend he wasn't my dog and carried on swimming. Fortunately, after a few more nervous minutes for both me and the hippie, he moved on, spotting a King Charles Spaniel farther down the beach and stealing its ball. This was a blessing in disguise as it eventually got me talking to the Spaniel's owner: a woman from Kent who recommended me two really good novels. Dog-borrowing had made this happen, and I was thankful for it.

With every week Billy and I became more comfortable about admitting the way we'd got together when we were talking to strangers while out walking. 'Us? Oh, we met on the Internet,' we'd announce confidently, in the knowledge that we lived in a brave new era when that sort of thing wasn't taboo any more. I noticed towards the end of July that Billy's profile was still active on borrowmydoggy.com, but I was sure it must have been just because he hadn't had time to take it down, since we'd agreed at the start of the month that we were now exclusive.

I genuinely believed that, by meeting Billy, I'd won the dog-borrowing lottery, so well suited was he to my walking needs, and so happy-go-lucky of temperament. Sure, I'd realised that there was a dastardly twinkle in his eye hiding under that stoner rock fringe, and that I had to keep him on the lead around sheep and cows, but I felt honoured by the excitement he seemed to feel when I picked him up from Susie's house. At weekends, he ran along Devon's beaches with vast packs of Susie's friends' dogs, as if he were living some idyllic *Chariots of Fire* dog dream, yet our considerably more sober walks, during which I would lecture him on cromlechs, Dartmoor folklore and Iron Age hill forts, still appeared to constitute an important part of his week, and I could not help but be touched and flattered by this.

Of course, it could be argued that borrowing a dog to walk was just greedy, when I already had at least one cat who would happily do the same thing any time I asked him. George's penchant for following me whenever I left the garden was increasing with every passing day, which was lovely, but, since I had no wish to be known in the village as That Guy Who Comes to the Post Office with His Cat, could also be a little inconvenient. The furthest he followed me was almost half a mile, up through the wild-flower meadow behind the house and along the unmetalled road back towards town, a purposeful look on his face the whole time, suggesting he believed we were fulfilling roles man and cat had occupied, side by side, for centuries. Leaving the house on foot began to necessitate all kinds of subterfuge. Seeing George come out of the cat flap behind me, I'd pull a face suggesting I'd forgotten an important document, head back inside then slip quietly out of the other door. I doubt, in retrospect, that George truly recognised the face that goes with realising you've forgotten an important document, but I felt it was best to make my ruse appear as all-round authentic as possible. At other times I'd deliberately time my trips out to coincide with his naps.

I loved the idea of walking with George, but the countryside behind the house was not quite the deserted landscape it had been in early spring: big dogs were regularly walked along the unmetalled lane, and the wild-flower meadow often served as a sunny day rendezvous point for bored adolescents. One hot afternoon I wandered over there to do some writing, followed by Ralph and George, then watched George saunter over and befriend a loved-up couple in their late teens, who proceeded to take a series of selfies with him. 'Somewhere out there, my new cat is on the Internet,' I thought. I felt sorry for George, who, as a rugged outdoorsman who'd been living off-grid, probably had no idea he was about to be put through a hipster Instagram filter, stamped with a hashtag and gawped at by dozens of strangers. Ralph, who'd been getting posted online for years accompanied by my mocking captions, knew better, and went off to hide in the hedgerow.

The quiet umbrage I took at the teenagers' brief theft of George was a measure of just how much I'd begun to think of him as 'my cat'. There was something very gratifying about knowing I'd rescued him from his feral lifestyle, then watched his appearance change: the scars on his ears and nose vanishing, his fur losing that dry quality which any rough-living cat's has, some soft, furry upholstery gradually appearing around his skinny ribs. He was impeccably behaved in and out of the house, to the extent that, even after four months of knowing him, Gemma and I had no actual evidence that he had bowel movements. He leapt on each of our laps in the evenings and stayed there, his only noises the sighs and whimpers that went with his apparently very involving cat dreams. When Shipley got in his face and insulted him, he flopped down submissively at his paws. It was as if he had taken care to use his homeless winter well, spying on other cat–human relationships and plotting the exact behaviour that would give him the maximum chance of being adopted on a long-term basis. It was impossible not to love him. Owing to this, directly after cuddling him I often found myself rushing over to the other cats and giving them fuss, to make sure they knew that they, as the 'lifers', were still the most important tenants here.

I didn't have to rush far in The Bear's case, since he was more often than not curled up next to George on the sofa or bed. Was this The Bear's amazing intuition regarding human behaviour at work again, telling him that he who had once seemed like a foe was now a friend? Or perhaps, being fundamentally of a generous and forgiving nature, he had just been quickly worn down by George's repeated attempts to be his mate.

The one area where George's plan to be The Perfect Cat fell short was Roscoe. If he'd only have left her alone, by this point we'd would have been giving him a gold-stamped lifetime membership card for the household, but his impulse to try to dry-hump her got the better of him time and time again. Any time he spotted her outside, he was in hot pursuit – often, troublingly, in the direction of the nearest traffic. Although the lane wasn't close to the house and was a quiet one, we feared for what might happen if George happened to chase Roscoe onto the tarmac at the wrong time. Mostly, Roscoe just hid. Because she'd always been something of a traveller, and was often away on business trips, it took us a while to realise just how much time she was spending out of the house. She'd lost weight, too; not a bad thing, perhaps, since last winter had been an indulgent one for her, causing Gemma to remark, not inaccurately at one point, 'Is it just me, or have you noticed how much our cat is starting to look like Kim Jong-un?'

For a while, Roscoe found refuge from George inside a

cupboard at the top of the stairs, but he soon managed to root her out. Alerted by a high-pitched noise redolent of a tiny, constipated demon, I'd run upstairs to find him standing over her as she pressed herself against the cupboard wall, upside down.

'HAVE YOU THOUGHT OF GETTING HER TO WEAR ONE OF THOSE MASKS YOU CAN GET WITH THE GOOFY TEETH, FALSE NOSE AND GLASSES?' suggested my dad. 'THEN GEORGE MIGHT FIND HER LESS ATTRACTIVE.'

Outside, the wild-flower meadow on the west side of the house and the unmetalled road and field behind it became George's territory, while Roscoe preferred to lie low in the undergrowth to the east that separated the house from a rushing granite stream, an alder and oak copse and The Torch beyond. At least, I assumed that's where she was hanging out, as it was where I most often found her, crouching in the long grass, on the days she didn't come home at mealtimes and I went looking for her. Roscoe was a cat who'd never enjoyed being picked up: a cat who, if cats wore T-shirts, would probably have worn one emblazoned with the slogan 'Too Cool for Cuddles' in fake graffiti lettering – but she seemed unusually glad to be whisked up into my arms at these points, as if relieved to have an escort to grant her safe passage past the ginger layabout who, like so many hippie men of the past, had cloaked his selfish carnal desires under the ostensibly well-meaning banner of 'free love'. When Roscoe wasn't around, George wandered about the place in a ubiquitous haze of easy-going affection and good intentions. Meanwhile, the precious morsels of affection Roscoe had offered me and Gemma in the past – very gently attempting to eat our hair, say, or leaping on us and padding us to within an inch of our lives whenever we were wearing a bath towel – began to peter out. It wasn't always easy for us, arguing the case for our aloof, irritable cat over our new, sociable, impossibly affable one, but we could see Roscoe's point: in her eyes, we had willingly invited a sex offender into the comfort of our own home.

There was a further indignity for Roscoe: she had lost her regular nap buddy to the very cat she most despised. To be fair to The Bear, he never seemed quite as comfortable sleeping next to George as he did next to Roscoe. 'This cat is an idiot!' his eyes seemed to say to me, when George attempted to nudge up to him on the sofa. 'I hope you realise I'm enduring this purely for your sake.' But even outside, The Bear, with the exception of Roscoe, was the cat George seemed most to want to be around, perhaps because he had worked out that, at the core of things, it was he, and not his louder stepbrothers, who pulled the strings behind the scenes on our whole operation. When The Bear wanted a break from George, he would invariably head off for a kip in what we'd come to know affectionately as 'The Bearhole': a circular, cat-shaped depression in the lawn beside a yew tree which he had made his own. George, who was getting bigger by the day, would not have managed to squeeze into The Bearhole with The Bear, so kept his distance, perhaps realising how jealously its proprietor guarded his sleep space. Before he slept in The Bearhole, often for periods of up to seven hours, The Bear would go around and around several times inside it, being sure to find the optimum resting position in the yew tree's shade.[2]

The Bearhole was one of two notable holes that had appeared in the garden over summer. The other was on the opposite side of the garden, and much deeper. When I'd first inspected it I'd found a wasp buzzing about in its furthest recesses. 'Wow,' I'd thought. 'Wasps are so good at digging!' But, as was confirmed to me later by Tristan Gooley, who'd got down on all fours and inspected it and sniffed the four small turds beside it, its more likely architect was a badger: Tristan could tell partly by the hole's shape, which resembled a capital 'D' that had fallen on its side.

Tristan, who is an expert in rural tracking and navigating using natural signs, was visiting me to assist with a newspaper column I was writing about countryside detective work. Soon the two of us set off down into the valley, with Tristan explaining how I could use daisies and the clouds as a compass, and, perhaps most surprisingly of all, which butterflies would tell me I was near a pub. George, who liked butterflies too, seemed keen to join us, and there was a bit of a delay while we gave him the slip. Tristan had walked in eclectic landscapes all over the globe and encountered many exotic creatures, but he would later admit that this was the first walk he'd ever been on where he had had to hide and then run away from a medium-sized domestic cat.

Later that week, on another lengthy walk with Billy, I

2 Also being quite old, male and living near a river, all he really needed was to have come from some islands off the West Coast of Ireland and he would have related completely to the lyrics of Nik Kershaw's 1984 hit song 'The Riddle'.

got the chance to put what I'd learned from Tristan into practice – a bit more of a chance than I'd anticipated, in fact. This walk, in retrospect, had not been one of my better pieces of planning. Excited by another beautiful Devon afternoon, a productive morning of writing and a slight improvement in my illness, I'd done what any sensible outdoorsy person who'd recently been weeing blood and running a high temperature would do in the same situation: hastily thrown an A–Z in my bag and set off, wearing very few clothes, to find a deep natural pool to swim in, high on Dartmoor. I'd memorised the first part of my seven-mile route and only reached for my A–Z after a couple of miles, turning to the appropriate grid reference and finding, to my puzzlement, a sewage works just outside of St Neots. It was at this point that I became fully aware of my predicament: a bare-legged, sockless man standing in the middle of one of the wildest expanses of land in the British Isles, possibly surrounded on all sides by adders, in burning hot sun, equipped with only a thimbleful of water, a small, ineffectual dog and a map of Cambridgeshire.

North, south, east and west are very different concepts in Devon to what they are in most places in the UK. The jagged dance of the coastline, the undulation of the land and the snaking nature of the rivers conspire to disorientate even the most geographically aware person. Usually I was verging on smug about my sense of direction, but standing there in the middle of the moor, on the bracken-overwhelmed ghost of a footpath, I couldn't have distinguished south from north on pain of death. There were a few hairy moments before, using what could perhaps best be described as 'an awareness of a slight distant dip in the landscape where some larger than average birds were swooping', I managed to navigate Billy and myself back to the river. It involved a lengthy detour, but I even found the pool I was looking for, eventually, and took a half-hour dip in it. As I did so, Billy let out an uncharacteristic bark, which I hoped wasn't dog for 'You do realise there's a rotting sheep's carcass just upstream from here, don't you?'

That night, Gemma and I went to The Torch for a drink and, somewhat exhaustedly, I recounted the day's adventure. I also told her that I'd seen the small water snake again that lived in our pond. I'd spotted this snake, whom I'd named Rick Snakeman, several times now, yet Gemma resolutely refused to believe in his existence.

'I'm telling you, he was there,' I said. 'He looked right at me and flicked his tongue.'

'I call bullshit,' said Gemma. 'I've looked all over that pond really carefully and there's no snake in it.'

'But I showed you a photo as proof. Snakeman is totally real.'

'That was just a blob. I saw no proof it was an actual snake.'

'This is so unfair.'

'Maybe it was the Totnes Monster that you saw.'

We sat there talking for at least ten minutes before we spotted Roscoe with some men on one of the other tables outside the pub. She appeared to be deep in conversation, so we were a little reluctant to interrupt at first, but eventually we called her over to where we were sitting.

'Roscoe!' shouted Gemma.

'Roscoe . . . ?' I echoed, a little less certainly.

Giving what looked like a 'Hold that thought, I'll be back!' gesture with one of her paws, Roscoe sashayed over in our direction. Her manner seemed somehow both embarrassed and confident. Kind of, 'OK, so I hid it from you for a while, and that was wrong, but I'm a strong, independent woman, and if you don't like it, there are plenty of people who will.'

'Is that your cat?' asked a lady at the table adjacent to us.

'I'm afraid so,' I said.

In the background, I could see the men Roscoe had been talking to – the kind of healthily weather-beaten, Rizla-smoking types you saw a lot of in Totnes and its surrounding villages – laughing and pointing in our direction.

'I'm sorry to tell you this, but it's not the first occasion,' said the lady. 'I've seen her up here a couple of times, rubbing herself against blokes.'

We finished our drinks and, feeling not unlike the concerned, square parents of a roaming, delinquent teenager, led Roscoe back home. I could feel the stifled giggles of the patrons of The Torch burning into my back. Roscoe maintained that same sashay as she followed us, as if full of new confidence, but the aura of self-possession vanished by the time we'd reached the garden, and she began to scuttle from bush to bush nervously, looking out for George, who, fortunately, was zonked out in my study, giving us time to feed her a classic post-pub meal of appalling mechanically recovered meat coated in jelly.

Discovering the secret side to our typically aloof cat – affable, gregarious, flirtatious – led to an evening of questions, most of which Gemma and I could only direct at ourselves. There were a few I wanted to direct at Roscoe too, though. Principal among them perhaps being: 'You're scared of the feline version of the Dude from *The Big Lebowski*, but you're not scared of total strangers in a pub?'

'I think maybe we just have to face up to the fact that George can't live here any more,' said Gemma. I was leaning, with extreme reluctance, towards the same conclusion, but had we really given it enough time? It had still only been a couple of months since George was neutered, and perhaps his hormones would die down. Maybe if we sat the two of them down together in a room, we could iron this whole thing out. Mostly, I just wished Roscoe would act as tough and nonchalant with him as she did with the other three cats: I was sure none of this was anything a couple of sharp bops to George's nose couldn't sort out.

The following week, on dog-borrowing day, I made a mistake. After Susie dropped Billy off, I'd left him outside and popped back into the house to get my walking boots, then remembered some bed sheets I needed to get out of the washing machine. As I'd been hanging them up to dry, I'd heard a commotion outside. I didn't actually see Roscoe, but something puffed up and eager in Billy's manner told me she'd been there. She'd developed a sixth sense regarding the times when George was asleep or not around, slinking cautiously up to the French windows and asking to be let in. Since George was currently on a rare adventure, and she had missed her meal the previous night, she'd probably felt this was the ideal moment to return, only to be chased down by an even dumber, even more overzealous tormentor. I mentally punched myself in the face. Could I have done anything more to alienate her and exacerbate her nerves?

Later that day, I scoured her favourite undergrowth and wandered over to The Torch, but there was no sign of her. By the time Gemma and I had gone to bed, Roscoe still hadn't arrived home. That night we barely got any rest, leaping out of bed to investigate at the slightest creak or bump of the house. When the Ralarm went off at five, I got straight up, as I knew I wasn't going to sleep any more anyway. I opened the bedroom door to a stunned Ralph, who stopped, mouth gaping, in mid-'Raaaaalph!' and stared up at me. Even he must have known something was wrong. 'You got up at my first Ralarm,' his look seemed to say. 'You never usually get up until at least my third Ralarm.'

That day I set off on a proper Roscoe hunt. This was not easy, due to George's ever-increasing determination to follow me each time I left the garden. After about six failed attempts, I ended up shutting him in the living room, but even then Shipley followed me outside, so an extra decoy of a bowlful of turkey chunks was required. I walked over to the next valley, then to the valley beyond that. Sound travelled in a confusing way in these hills; what you thought was the sound of a cat was often not a cat. I had learned this the previous month when I had mistakenly attempted to whistle an elderly Spanish tourist in for some mass-produced trout coated in gravy. Now, calling Roscoe, I sometimes thought I heard her high-pitched *ewew*, but when I listened again it seemed to blur and drown in a cacophony of birdsong, rushing water and wind-rustled fronds. I asked up at the pub and knocked on the door of a couple of neighbours, but nobody had seen a small black and white cat. Admittedly, Gemma and I received this vanishing act somewhat differently to how we would have taken one from The Bear, Shipley, Ralph or even George. All of them were total homebodies and, if they'd been away this long, we'd have been crawling up the walls. Nonetheless, by the time we went to bed that night, it had been over fifty hours since we'd last seen Roscoe, and we were beginning to seriously worry.

It wasn't until the next morning that I finally spotted her, after driving Gemma to the station to get her train to work. At least, I thought it was Roscoe. I was about a mile away from the house at the time, at the edge of the village, next to a group of Victorian terraces and some marshland near the river. The flurry of black and white fur I saw through the corner of the windscreen was brief, but something about its businesslike nature told me it was her. I stopped the car, but the high-banked lane was especially narrow here, and parking was dangerous, so I quickly drove home then returned on foot. I revisited the same spot three more times during the day and whistled myself hoarse, but there was no Roscoe. That evening, Gemma and I went back to the same spot again and whistled and called some more. Eventually, a cat emerged from one of the gardens of the Victorian terraces, perhaps impressed by our persistence and wondering if it meant that we were nicer to cats than its present owners and would therefore be better to live with. It was an extremely lovely cat, which looked like a small lion, and, for the next twenty minutes of our search, it shadowed our every move. If we were being honest, we would both have been elated to take it home and let it manipulate us, but it was important to stay disciplined and stick to the task at hand.

Could Roscoe have really wandered that far? To get there, she'd have had to cross a road, negotiate some thick woodland and a wide stream. I will probably never know for sure, but that evening when, on a last desperate search of the day in the fading light, she finally came back, it was from that direction she came. She scuttled towards me down the path behind the garden, wide-eyed and frantically *ewew*ing, as if she was at the end of a long and confusing journey. She made uncharacteristically little protest when I picked her up, and Gemma and I would later agree that it was the first time ever that we'd seen her looking tired.

After feeding her and taking her up to the bedroom, where she could have a long sleep out of George's reach, one of the first things I did was text my mum to let her know we'd found her. She and my dad had adopted Floyd at the same time we'd adopted Roscoe, and we'd been comparing and contrasting their progress ever since: Floyd's evolution from a hyperactive kitten who liked to play 'fetch' to a juvenile delinquent; Roscoe's from a tiny she-devil in a Batman mask to a confident business-woman. My mum had been having her own sleepless nights about Floyd recently, who was straying farther and farther into the countryside surrounding their house, and could sympathise with our plight.

I hadn't spoken to my parents properly for a while. I

told my mum I missed them, and suggested we skyped and had a proper catch-up the following day. We'd never done this before, typically preferring to communicate using the old-fashioned landline method, and my mum seemed surprised, though not unhappy, at the suggestion. Perhaps by this point she already sensed there might be an ulterior motive involved. I'm not sure. But she's a wise woman, so she quickly got the full picture the following day when she opened her iPad and accepted my call, to find me sitting on the sofa, with George upside down on my lap.

'So I was wondering,' I said. 'How would you feel about adopting another cat?'

# Cat Lists

**Pros of Taking In a Stray Cat**

Grateful for food.
  Few stray cats vote UKIP.
  Easy to please with birthday presents (e.g., leaf, button).

**Cat names that are now so over**

Chairman Meow
  Evelyn Paw
  Gary

**Cat names trending for the new season**

Pussolini
  Doris
  Uncle Fuckykins

## Ways to Annoy Your Cat On Facebook

Repeatedly invite your cat to play Candy Crush Saga.

Like the comments underneath your cat's status but never the actual status itself.

Always add a small 'x' when tagging mice in your status but not when tagging your cat.

Always eat vegetarian at home but post plenty of photos of large elaborate meat-based meals you've had while out.

## Good Reasons to get a Black Cat

Often unfairly overlooked at rescue centres.

Read lots more books than cats of other colours.

Hair doesn't show up on clothes if you're a goth.

Very slimming to hug.

## Telltale Signs Your Cat might be Overgrooming

Cat comes in with old spider webs and moss and twigs stuck to its fur, but in a way that seems a bit too studied and deliberate.

Cat cannot go out without being dissed and called a meowtrosexual by rough feral cats.

Bathroom sink often flecked with loose whiskers/tiny pairs of tweezers.

Cat begins to catch fewer mice, due to noticing its reflection in windows on way to catch mice and stopping to check itself out.

## Ideas for Potential Children's Books Inspired by My Cats

The Cat Who got a bit Mardy then Ate a Hare
   Slug Cat Goes on a Big Adventure
   The Cat Who Meowed Mournfully at a Bowl of Water for No Apparent Reason
   Owl and Cat are Largely Indifferent to One Another
   The Cat Who Fucked an Ikea Blanket

# He's Got Eyes

I'd thrown myself into Devon life with so much zest since moving that I'd begun to forget, to an extent, that it wasn't a country entirely of its own. In five months I'd not left the county once, nor felt any real desire to do so. Now, on my first trip out, it came as something of a shock to arrive back in civilisation – or Somerset, as it was sometimes also called – in barely over an hour. The traffic remained clear until Weston-super-Mare, when we ground to a halt. Cars moving in the opposite direction appraised our gridlock from the other carriageway, no doubt experiencing that particular smug motorway emotion that should be known as 'Strassenfreude'. A fluorescent-striped highway maintenance vehicle zipped down the hard shoulder parallel to us: a hoverfly to the traffic police's wasps. I looked from a bemused, alien perspective at this flustered, sighing world of slick company cars, M&S, Costa and Welcome Break outlets and well-ironed shirts on back-seat hangers. George, who had almost certainly never seen it before, was surely more bemused still. He panted slightly in the heat, and I cracked the window and put on *Homecoming*, the second album by the laid-back country rock band America, for him. This America album didn't include the band's most famous song, 'A Horse With No Name', but I liked it even more, and it was similarly mellow and George-friendly. It got me thinking about the most bizarre detail surrounding 'A Horse With No Name', which was that, despite being one of the most American songs of 1971, it was recorded in Puddletown in Dorset, about eighty miles south-east of our current traffic jam, a fact that, ever since I'd discovered it, caused me to hear the line 'in the desert, you can remember your name' as 'in the Dorset, you can remember your name'.

'Is it just me,' said my mum, turning to check on George in the back seat, 'or does he look like he's smiling?'

'Oh, George is always smiling,' I said. 'Also, America are one of his very favourite bands, right up there alongside Crosby, Stills and Nash and The Beach Boys.'

'I'm afraid he's probably not going to hear much of that at our house. Your dad's going through quite a big Timbaland phase at the moment.'

To further pass the time, as we remained stationary, my mum told me about a troubling encounter she'd had outside her house recently involving two hedgehogs. 'I heard a very frightening noise in the night and went outside to see if Floyd was being murdered, or was murdering something, and two big hedgehogs were slugging it out on the lawn. Then one turned on me and attacked my fluffy slippers. I was really scared!'

I suggested that perhaps, in an adrenaline-fuelled red mist, the hedgehog had mistaken my mum's slippers for a couple of hipster hedgehogs with fancy ideas about grooming who needed to be taken down a peg or two. It went to show that the British countryside is fraught with peril, and the very objects we assume will protect us can turn against us in a heartbeat. Even a slipper – warm and reassuring, so often the shield between the cat-owning rural dweller and a cold kitchen floor or mouse spleen – could be the very thing that puts us most in jeopardy. Yet ultimately I found my mum's story slightly comforting. All through the journey so far I'd been feeling bad for dragging George away from his cat Utopia, and it reminded me that he was travelling to another very rural area, with lots of green space and nature around him.

In the end, it took us six and a quarter hours to reach the far end of Nottinghamshire: two more than we'd anticipated. The plan was that I'd drop off my mum, who'd come down on the train from Devon a couple of days earlier, and George and then stick around for a night to help him settle in. All being well, I'd proceed to north Norfolk, where I was scheduled to speak at a literary festival. In quintessentially awkward feline fashion, George had chosen the morning of our journey to adopt a live-and-let-live attitude to Roscoe for the first time in weeks, remaining supine on the living room floorboards as she scuttled nervously past the window, but we had to stick to the plan now. 'Once he's settled in, he'll probably be happier there anyway,' Gemma and I told each other. I'm not sure I believed it, but I wanted to. The one issue was Floyd, but he seemed to get on well with other cats. His relationship with Casper had progressed from an innocent adolescent wrestling club to a rough-and-tumble adult friendship with an unhealthy controlling aspect to it, courtesy of Floyd, but it did not result in any serious physical harm to Casper. 'It's only rodents and humans Floyd seems to injure,' said my mum, showing me the latest puncture wound in her nose.

'HE'S UPSTAIRS AT THE MOMENT, PASSED OUT ON THE BED,' said my dad when we arrived. 'HE'S BEHEADED FOUR VOLES IN THE LAST DAY, SO HE'S REALLY TIRED. AND HE ATTACKED THE PRINTER AGAIN.' My mum and dad's computer printer was Floyd's latest obsession; any time he heard it in use, he'd race towards it and jam his paw into it.

'I DOUBT HE'LL BE UP FOR AGES.' My dad looked at George. 'IS THAT OUR NEW CAT? ALL RIGHT, OUR KID. BLOODY HELL, HE'S BIG, ISN'T HE?'

On being released from his carrier, George made an immediate beeline for the space behind the wood burner, where he retrieved a dead mouse covered in dust. The move was carried out with stunning determination and precision. It was almost as if at some point during the car journey George had clandestinely received a text on a tiny cat phone from a secret agent cat, which read: 'Your first mission on arrival will be to retrieve a deceased rodent. This is located in the fireplace and has been deceased for four days. Your mission is to be carried out in no longer than twenty-seven seconds. Over.'

'FOOKTIVANO!' said my dad. 'HOW DID HE KNOW THAT WAS THERE? THAT MAKES IT FOURTEEN THAT FLOYD'S KILLED THIS WEEK.'

As George mooched about and familiarised himself with the remainder of the downstairs of the house, my mum, my dad and I sat down to eat. Among other dishes, my dad had made a delicious-looking mackerel salad. I explained that I had been vacillating between a vegetarian and pescatarian diet recently, and was currently in a fish-free phase. My dad waved this suggestion away. 'GERRIT DOWN YOU. DON'T WORRY ABOUT IT. ANYWAY, MACKEREL DON'T HAVE FEELINGS. THEY'VE PROVED IT.'

Twenty minutes later, while my mum and I cleared the dishes away, we heard a telltale jingle and Floyd appeared on the stairs, with a sleepy-eyed but suspicious look. I'd never thought of Floyd as having a harsh face in the past, but, thanks to the time I'd spent looking at George's beatific, kind one, there seemed something a little cruel about it now. This was emphasised a few minutes later when Floyd, seeing George, immediately pounced on him and lamped him repeatedly on the head.

I'm aware that there are specific guidelines it's wise to follow when introducing a new cat into a household where another cat already lives. Experts believe you should keep the cats apart for a lengthy period of time, using clothing or blankets to get them gradually accustomed to one another's smell. But I'd brought George a long, long way, very reluctantly, and I wanted to get a sense that he was OK before I left him. After a small break, a second introduction was even less successful, with Floyd pouncing on George in much the same way as a fascist policeman with his blood up might have pounced on a peaceful hippie protesting the Vietnam War. How had I not noticed in the past just how long and sharp Floyd's claws were? A third introduction, the following morning, was an almost exact replay of the scene where Bruce Lee fights Han and his terrifying metal claw, the only difference being that, in this case, instead of doing spectacular kung fu kicks on Han, Bruce Lee cowered in a corner looking scared, confused and alone.

'Perhaps this isn't going to work,' said my mum.

'IT'S BREAKING MY HEART,' said my dad, picking George up. 'I'VE GOT AN IDEA: WHAT IF WE KEEP GEORGE AND YOU TAKE FLOYD BACK WITH YOU? IF HE DOESN'T LIKE IT THERE HE CAN ALWAYS GO UP AND LIVE ON HIS OWN ON DARTMOOR. HE'D BE OK, AND HE'D HAVE NO PROBLEM FINDING FOOD. IF HE GOT HUNGRY HE'D JUST BRING DOWN ONE OF THE PONIES UP THERE.'

It was with extreme reluctance later that morning that I said goodbye to George and set off for Norfolk. 'Maybe things will improve,' said my mum. 'Don't worry. We'll keep you informed of how it's going. Try to relax and have a good time.'

'WATCH OUT FOR FOOKWITS AND LOONIES,' said my dad. 'AND FOR SNAKES.'

'You haven't still got that one in your car, have you?' I asked.

'YEAH. IT'S REALLY SHRIVELLED FROM THE HEAT NOW, THOUGH. THERE'S ALMOST NONE OF IT LEFT. I MIGHT THROW IT AWAY SOON.'

'No need to rush these things, though, is there? Why not wait a few more months?'

'YOU'RE PROBABLY RIGHT.'

Norfolk had its own colour in the August heat: a sand-blasted yellow, sharply in contrast to Devon's endless greens. Driving in from the north coast, where I'd done my spoken word event, Norwich felt as familiar and welcome as a tasty pizza slice you've forgotten you've left in the fridge the night before. In its Golden Triangle district, the cats were typically out in force.

'We saw Gingersaurus last week,' my friends Drew and Jecca told me, 'but it's been ages since we saw Crybaby Hedgecat.' Though not cat owners themselves, Drew and Jecca were careful to track the comings and goings of the cats of the neighbourhood, giving them their own names. Walking from their Victorian terrace back into town, I was pleased to see a familiar, cowlike cat I'd tried to befriend the previous year sitting in his customary position in the middle of the pavement, watching traffic. But witnessing these confident city cats, at one with their environment, I could not help thinking of George, anything but at one with his, sitting bewildered on my mum and dad's sofa before I left.

Though sparsely attended, the literary festival at which

I'd read had been fun, and turned out to be the spring-board for a weekend of much bigger fun: one of those rare periods where the sun is shining non-stop, you've got nothing arduous arranged and have managed to gather many of your favourite people in the world in one place. Sitting in beer gardens and flicking through shelves of second-hand books and records, though, I found that George was never far from my thoughts. When I woke up in Drew and Jecca's spare bed, his plaintive meow – 'Geeeeeooooorge', the meow that had greeted me at the bottom of the stairs every morning, without fail, since the day I'd brought him back from the vet's – rang in my ears, with just the hint of a guilt-inducing question mark on its final note. Text updates arrived from my mum's iPad but they were not promising ('Another meeting, Floyd scratched George's nose, George back locked in bedroom, looking depressed . . .') and all the time here I was, drinking ale and eating chilli-coated chips and having the weekend of my life. 'What a heartless bastard I am!' I thought.

I'd rescued cats before, winning the trust of a cat who was living wild and inviting him to live in your house brought with it a slightly different set of emotions to adopting a cat from a shelter. Being away from George in another place highlighted what a unique bond I'd forged with him: not something better than the one I'd forged with any of my other cats, but something close and trust-ing in an entirely different way. I thought about the way George followed me; the possessive way he thwacked his tail against me when we went on walks together; the way seeing his gentle, peaceful face every morning gave me a sense of well-being; a feeling that, despite the world being a messed-up place, and life being full of struggle, everything was intrinsically OK.

I'd owed Roscoe a break from his attentions, but I felt I owed George more than this. Being out at work in the day, Gemma had not forged the same bond with him, but, after I called her from Norwich and explained the situation with Floyd, she shared my opinion: maybe the course of action we'd taken wasn't the right one after all. The decision was made, but perhaps it had truly been made a couple of days earlier, when I first arrived at my mum and dad's house with George. So, when I'd said goodbye to my friends in Norwich, I did not point my car in a south-westerly direction, as originally planned, but back in the north-westerly one I had arrived from.

I would not precisely have described George as 'happy' during our trip back to Devon, and the stretch of the journey between Walton on the Wolds and Leicester Forest East Services was characterised by some frantic *Geeeeooooorge*ing, but he seemed to calm down when I put Jackson Browne's debut album on, and his overall equanimity through his four-day ordeal had been amazing to behold. Released back into his former home, he sauntered into the living room and flopped on my battered old leather sofa as if he'd been no farther than his favourite local meadow. 'I don't mind,' his attitude seemed to say. 'It's all better than being homeless.' His attitude was notably more humble than Shipley's, who, arriving in the living room and seeing George's return, let out a profanity so loud and obscene I found myself wanting to attach a parental advisory tag to his collar in addition to the two bells that currently hung there.

George's return came with a strict proviso, which I assured Gemma I would remain diligently responsible for: that it was my job – even above any of my actual jobs, which paid the rent and bills – to go to every length possible to keep him and Roscoe apart. My routine was the same every morning: feed George, The Bear, Ralph and Shipley, shut George in the dining room, head up to the undergrowth behind the house, call Roscoe, find Roscoe

in a bush, take Roscoe back home, feed Roscoe, wait for Roscoe to head up to the bedroom to sleep, let George out of the dining room. If I was determined and disciplined enough and limited my trips out of the house, I could almost create the illusion for George and Roscoe that each other didn't exist. It was hard work, and it wasn't exactly what you'd call 'a Life', but I tried to look at it from a George kind of perspective: at least it was better than being homeless.

There was no period of readjustment for George: he was instantly back to his old ways here, following me on walks, languidly chasing butterflies and purring at the hillside's thriving bumblebee population. That was perhaps unsurprising, since this place had been his home before – perhaps long before – it had been ours. His one baffling fear had always been the cupboard beneath our stairs. Each time I opened it when George was around, his face became a mask of bug-eyed terror and he'd flee to another part of the house. I wondered if this was because it was where I kept my old metal clothes horse – a contraption that had been a nemesis of Ralph's for well over a decade – but on the occasions I took the clothes horse out of the cupboard, George was entirely nonchalant about it. I sensed there was another, much more deep-seated story here. With the exception of Floyd, the cupboard was the only thing I'd ever seen George genuinely terrified of. Perhaps the house's previous occupants had kept George locked in the cupboard, like a feline Harry Potter? Maybe the cupboard had its own ghost? I gave the latter theory most credence: so much so, in fact, that once when I went into the cupboard to get the vacuum cleaner, and the ironing board fell over behind me, briefly wedging the door shut, I went into my own George-style panic.

Overlooking the diligence and time that was required to keep him and Roscoe segregated, George remained an effortless cat to be around. When he was on my lap, he made none of Ralph or Shipley's wriggling, possessive demands. He was calm and still. His plush coat was now a pleasure to stroke, smoothly radiating good health. When he looked up at me with a question in his eyes, it was always one that seemed to call for a simple answer, as opposed to the complex, moralistic one demanded by The Bear on similar occasions. Yet he had his mysterious side, too; his easy domestication masked some ingrained, clandestine feral habits. Driving away from home one day, Gemma and I were shocked to glance over a hedge five or six hundred yards from the house and see him prowling purposefully through a field in the direction of some barns belonging to our local farm. This suggested that the obedient imminence of George's arrivals when I whistled him in for food was less down to his proximity to the house at the time and more to the acuteness of his hearing and speed of his strong legs.

On another occasion I opened the back gate and found him behind the hedge, shyly crunching through the last vestiges of a mouse. This was so different to the approach of Shipley and Ralph, who invariably brought their mice in, played volleyball with them then left them quarter-eaten or whole. There was something very feral about

the ideology behind it: rodent purely as sustenance, rather
than present or plaything. I hoped this wouldn't change,
since Shipley and Ralph had really been putting the work
in, rodent-wise, recently. Their new bells had put a stop
to the rabbit slaughter, but the fact that when in pursuit
of prey each of them made the noise of a small upbeat
church seemed to make no difference to the mouse and
vole kill count. At certain times of the night the area
around the dining room resembled a vole racetrack. I
managed to catch and free most of the voles, but it was
starting to cut severely into my free time. Then there
were those I failed to spot, such as the one rotting behind
the fridge and another I found crushed as flat as a pressed
flower beneath a fallen picture frame.[3]

By far Shipley's most alarming kill of recent days was a
full-sized adult hare. Shipley was an astonishingly deft
and speedy sprinter for his advancing years, but hares can
really put a clip on, and I concluded the poor thing must
already have been very ill, if not dying, in order for him to
catch it. There was something far more shocking about
seeing him arrive in the garden with it than seeing him
earlier in the year with rabbits in his mouth. It left me
feeling like I'd just watched a friend I thought I knew
gun down a kindly wizard in cold blood.

Back in June I'd been talking to a yoga instructor in the
village called Sue, who was closely connected to someone

---

3 Incidentally, if you have ever pondered the question, 'Where do a
vole's innards go when it is crushed flat beneath a fallen picture frame?'
I can confirm first-hand that the answer is, 'They vanish magically into
thin air.'

who ran something she called a 'touring taxidermy peep show'. I wasn't sure of the exact details, but the gist of it seemed to be that dead animals dressed up in, then took off, a range of Victorian clothes in front of a small crowd of people who'd tired of regular ways to have fun. I thought now of Sue, who often stored badgers, rabbits and foxes for her friend in the large fridge in her garage, but I could not bring myself to phone or text her. This dignified creature in front of me on the lawn surely deserved a less tacky afterlife than being repeatedly cracked onto by a horny fox in a top hat. Yet somehow leaving it in a quiet place beneath the bracken and nettles behind the garden, as I usually did with rabbits and voles, didn't seem quite distinguished enough, so instead I fetched a spade from the garden shed, dug a small hole in the same area and buried it there. The whole procedure took around an hour, which, going on usual cat schedules, left me about forty-five minutes of working time before George made his next attempt to sexually harass Roscoe.

Early evening was always a danger time in terms of the George and Roscoe situation: Roscoe would have asked to come out of the bedroom by this point. George too would be waking up, and we'd often be off our guard, busy with the preparation of dinner and other jobs. One night in August as Gemma and I sat down to eat, I heard a commotion outside and exploded out of the back door, expecting to discover George arched over Roscoe, only to find The Bear and George watching a badger run industriously across the lawn. I'd lived almost my entire life in the countryside, but this was the first badger I'd ever seen up close, and I was excited. I was also interested to note that badgers don't run like the other wild, four-legged animals of Britain; they run a bit like a garish 1970s foot-stool might run if it suddenly realised it had the power of functioning limbs. I got the impression this one had been hanging around a fair bit recently, and the sight of it came as a relief, suggesting to me that some of the 'knock-ing over bins and plant pots' noises we'd heard in the night over the last two weeks had not actually been down to an alcoholic hobo, as I'd previously feared. The Bear, George and I watched the badger as it scuttled past its hole and then, perhaps seeing that the hole was still occu-pied by the same wasp who'd been there last month, vanished into the hedge.

The Bear and George continued to spend a lot of time together. When they slept on the sofa or the bed, George would gradually edge closer backwards towards The Bear, until The Bear appeared to be more or less spooning him. 'Aren't you both sweet!' I'd say, finding them like this, and The Bear would look up at me with the tired, long-suffering eyes of someone doomed to live for ever in the company of simpletons.

Had The Bear ever truly had a friend of his own species: a cat fully on his level? I remembered hearing rumours of playmates in his early years, back when he lived with my ex's ex in the suburbs of east London, but I'd never seen evidence of them. I liked to imagine that the answer to his solitude would be to forge a bond with one of the owls who lived in the hills around Totnes. There was certainly no shortage of them. Sometimes there were so many *woo-woos* in the area immediately beyond the garden it felt like being in the middle of an illegal rave. There were tuneful owls and more discordant owls, perhaps in the middle of working on their difficult second owlbums. The tuneful owls dominated, which suggested that the number of male tawnies in the area heavily outnumbered the number of females. Surely an elderly, slightly asexual one of these single owl gentlemen could find something in common with The Bear? I pictured the two of them reading poetry to one another, then turning in to sleep the sleep of the learned and wise on separate bookshelves, each equipped with their own nightlight.

I'd always suspected that, along with 'academic', 'poet'

and 'diplomat', 'owl' must have been one of The Bear's jobs in a previous life. Owls, I felt, were one of the few types of animal who shared his quiet, watchful intelligence. However, I was swiftly disabused of this notion by Jordan, one of the owl handlers I met on a visit to Totnes Rare Breeds Farm. 'They're actually one of the world's thickest animals,' he told me.

'So all that stuff you hear about owls having their own offices in important universities and being able to read *Ulysses* all the way through in one weekend is nonsense?' I asked.

'Yep, I'm afraid so. They've got big eyes and a very small head, which leaves very little room for brain.'

'Their hearing is amazing, though,' added Sam, the farm manager who worked with Jordan. 'Many of these owls can hear a mouse's heartbeat from two metres away.'

I'd decided to visit the Rare Breeds Farm after chatting to Pete, the man I frequently saw walking a European eagle owl around Totnes. The owl, an exquisite creature with a wingspan big enough to carry a dozen hardback books it would never read, was called Wizard, and was in fact one of three owls from the farm who Pete regularly took out for a walk. The other two were a Siberian eagle owl called Merlin and Pete's own winged companion, a great grey owl named Lady Jane Grey. Pete had once owned a haulage firm in Yorkshire, but, having visited a friend in Devon and really enjoyed looking after some donkeys for a fortnight, went straight back home, sold his company, moved south-west and began to volunteer at the Rare Breeds Farm, which is also home to alpacas, red squirrels, pot-bellied pigs and angora goats. A good example of the amazing hearing of the owls, Sam told me, was that Lady Jane Grey could always hear Pete's fourteen-year-old Rover 75 pull into the car park, and would get 'very excited at the sound of the engine'.

'I get all sorts of reactions walking around town with the owls,' Pete told me. 'One time I was out with Merlin and a lady asked me what kind of owl he was. I told her he was a Siberian eagle owl, and she immediately burst into tears. It turned out that she was from Siberia too, and missed it a lot. The owls seem to love coming out with me. Wizard especially likes the attention. The only problem is that it's difficult for me to go out into town on my own now without somebody stopping me and asking, "Why haven't you got an owl with you?"'

On the second occasion I'd stopped to chat with Pete on the outskirts of Totnes, not far from the 'Twinned with Narnia' town sign, which had since been amended to 'Twinned with Area 51', he'd asked Wizard to 'wave' goodbye to me, which Wizard duly did, using his wings. A couple of weeks later, I'd accompanied Pete and Lady Jane Grey on a wander around the town on market day, and we'd been stopped every three steps by people of all shapes, sizes, genders and nationalities. At one point, a flock of Spanish tourists mobbed us in a shop doorway, Lady Jane perched on Pete's arm, high on some steps above the throng, proudly posing for their iPhone photos like a newly acquitted defendant before a slathering media scrum after a high-profile court case.

At the Rare Breeds Farm, Sam let me into the enclosure and I had a circumspect cuddle with Wizard, being careful to keep clear of his talons, which, she told me, could go through nineteen-gauge steel. European eagle owls vanished from Britain for a while but have recently returned to the wild in small numbers. Forced to fend for himself, Wizard could easily spear himself a calf, a sheep or a small deer for dinner, but subsisted quite happily here on a slightly less adventurous diet.

All the owls at the Rare Breeds Farm were either rescue

owls or owls born in captivity. After Wizard, I met Flitwick, a little owl who preferred to sit on the fence of the enclosure due to 'liking to be stroked', and Queenie, a nervous barn owl rescued from some Harry Potter fans who'd kept her shut in a wardrobe for two years. On the list of awkward conversation topics to avoid with a barn owl, J. K. Rowling is right up there with Hooters restaurants, rodenticides and the episodes of the TV show *Grand Designs* that have centred around the conversion of draughty old farm buildings.

'Harry Potter has a lot to answer for,' said Sam. 'People buy barn owls over the Internet for their kids because they've watched the films, but they don't have any idea how to look after them. They're not pets, and shouldn't be treated that way.'

Sam had her own barn owl, Jake – whose impressively choreographed flying skills she later demonstrated for me – but Jake lived at the farm in his own aviary, not at her house, and Sam did not kid herself that he looked at her as anything more than a source of food.

I told Sam and Jordan about the wild owls I'd witnessed nearby: the little owls I'd seen sitting on fence posts in the morning, judging me as I emptied the recycling, and the rodent slaughter in the trees and scrub behind my house: a tawny version of the Totnes Good Food Market with the added bonus that it was held every night, not just the third Sunday of every month. Neither of them seemed surprised, and they told me that these same local wild tawnies were often known to bring 'presents' to the tame show owls at the Rare Breeds

Farm: a shrew here, half a rat or two there. The consensus among the Rare Breeds staff was that these gifts were either sex bribes or a manifestation of the tawnies' worries that Wizard, Merlin and friends weren't eating properly.

I preferred to believe the second of these explanations, just as I preferred to continue believing that owls were bright creatures, and that the many who had congregated in the hills around Totnes had come here for a reason. I could picture it clearly: an owl from a humdrum place who feels a bit misunderstood is flying around, feeling a bit rootless. She sees the 'Totnes: Twinned With Area 51' sign. 'Hmm, interesting,' she thinks, flying on, past a group of retirees on a wild food walk, a poster advertising a ten-week evening class exploring Woman's relationship with the moon and the Harlequin bookshop, run by Paul, who used to go out with Joan Baez. The owl swoops down and lands at the Rare Breeds Farm where, after saying a tentative hello to one of the angora goats that look like Roger Daltrey from The Who, she arrives at the aviary housing Wizard, Merlin and Lady Jane Grey and gives them the once-over. 'Bloody hell,' she says to herself. 'There are some strange-looking folks who live here. But I like it.'

It might be said that the owls who had settled near our cottage had made an even wiser property decision. Due to the proximity of Roscoe, Ralph and Shipley, these nocturnal predators had a whole extra food supply they didn't even have to go to the effort to kill themselves: a twitchell's worth of quarter-chewed voles, shrew faces and half-rabbits. They no longer even had to compete for these offcuts with the jackdaws on top of the chimney, who'd long since moved on. Sometimes, of course, these mangled body parts ended up indoors, out of the owls' reach, but, having cleared them up and scrubbed the carpet, I'd always place them behind the fence in what I'd come to think of as 'Owl Alley'.

Life must have been so simple for people without cats who got other people to look after their houses. All they had to say was stuff like, 'the shower is playing up a bit', 'the heating comes on at six in the morning and again at five in the evening' and 'make sure you give the umbrella plant in the dining room extra water'. There was no 'try to stop the foul-mouthed wiry black cat stealing the other cats' food', 'keep the drinking bowl in the bathroom topped up and don't be freaked out when the other black one meows at it as if he's in love with it', or 'if you find a mouse's bum on the carpet, just use some kitchen roll to pick it up, then pop it behind the back fence' for them. My mysterious river disease, which had escalated into prostatitis a few weeks earlier, and the increasing demands of my part-time job as a bodyguard for Roscoe, had left me more homelocked recently. Now I was feeling a bit better I needed a break, and Gemma and I were due to attend Drew and Jecca's wedding at the far end of Cornwall at the end of August. Asking any of our friends to look after our house, though, seemed a huge imposition: effectively the equivalent of requesting that they perform a short stint as unpaid janitors at a tiny abattoir. Then on top of that there was the Roscoe and George problem, the resurfacing of Shipley's predawn bin-kicking sessions and Ralph's increasingly loud and abrasive snoring, which, despite my countless hints, he refused to seek help for.

Fortunately, my dad, who offered to look after the cottage for us while we were away at the wedding, lived with Floyd, and had plenty of recent experience of dead rodents. But, for all the blood spatter he left around the house, Floyd rarely discarded actual body parts on the floor, and my dad was not known for his care and stealth when walking around the house in the early hours. I could not help thinking here of the incident a little more than a year ago, when, staying in my old spare room and allowing my mum and dad the use of my (much comfier) bed, I'd been woken in the night by an almighty crash. The next morning I'd asked my mum if she'd heard it too.

'Oh, er, yes,' she replied. 'That was your dad. He was on his way to the bathroom but ended up trying to get into your wardrobe instead.'

Then there was George. Could I reasonably expect my dad to repeat even half the complex drill I performed every day to keep him from dry-humping Roscoe? The brief locking of George in the dining room. The vigilant listening out for Roscoe by the living-room windows, and the particular times of day when it was most important to do so. The places where she would and wouldn't comfortably eat. The patches of undergrowth and parts of the pub where you were most likely to find her when she went missing.

'I'm sure it will be OK,' said my mum. 'Just make sure you leave lots of instructions. Your dad could really do with the break. He's been spending far too much time composting recently. He brought some really old compost back from next door's garden yesterday. He calls it "black gold" because it's so good. He smelt like a guinea pig after he'd used it.'

On the night he arrived, my dad decided to have a bath, and emerged from the bathroom half an hour later wrapped in all four of the remaining clean towels in the house. 'I'VE JUST SPRAYED MY HAIR WITH CONTACT LENS CLEANER,' he announced. 'I THOUGHT IT WAS MY HAIR SPRAY, BUT IT WAS CONTACT LENS CLEANER.'

This didn't fill me confidence for the three days to come, but there was no changing our minds now: we'd confirmed our presence at the wedding, booked our room at the venue and bought booze and presents to take with us. There would be no phone reception or wi-fi at the big old Gothic house where the wedding was being held, which was tucked away on a secluded cove a few miles outside Penzance, and if my dad needed to contact us, he'd be required to call the one phone there: an old 1960s dial-it-yourself contraption far away from any of the main rooms in the building, suggesting that hearing its old-fashioned tring would be impossible.

Once we were in Cornwall, though, these concerns

soon melted away into a mindful, other-worldly weekend of sea swimming, rocky coastal path walks, food, drink and dancing. It was only on the third day when I scrambled a mile back up the hill to the road to buy a pasty that my phone buzzed to life, revealing an email my dad had sent the previous evening. Written entirely in his customary capital letters, the message was direct and to the point:

WENT FOR A WALK AND FELL OFF A WALL AND COULDN'T GET UP 'CAUSE MY BACKPACK WAS SO HEAVY. MISTOOK A SHEEP TRACK FOR THE SOUTH DEVON COASTAL PATH AND NEARLY WALKED OFF A CLIFF EDGE. WENT FOR ANOTHER WALK WHILE THEY WERE DOING MY TAKEAWAY THEN COULDN'T FIND MY WAY BACK TO THE FOOKIN' PLACE. ALSO SHIPLEY PISSED IN MY SHORTS WHEN I WAS ASLEEP* AND GEORGE TRIED TO NOB ROSCOE BUT I WAS BETWEEN THEM IN A FLASH.
    *LUCKILY I WASN'T WEARING THEM AT THE TIME.

I suppose he might conceivably have had a better time, but I was relieved to hear that there had been no major disasters. The biggest relief of all was that Roscoe had not done another of her vanishing acts. On arriving back at the cottage, we found it mostly intact, overlooking a few towels and chocolate wrappers strewn around the place and a text from my mum that popped up on my phone later that day informing me that my dad had 'brought four of your pillowcases home by mistake'. George bounded down the garden path to greet us, thumping his tail against my legs in typically possessive fashion. Shipley, The Bear and Ralph followed, at a somewhat grudging distance, and Roscoe arrived an hour later, low to the ground, watching all the angles for a potential ambush.

I'd missed George while we were away – missed him as much as I could miss any cat of my own – but in the days that followed it became clear that his enthusiasm for Roscoe was not, as I'd hoped, cooling; in fact, quite the opposite. I still mostly succeeded in keeping them apart. However, as long as I was in the house and making any attempt to get on with my life, it would never be long before I heard her banshee alarm noise. Rushing to the rescue, I'd usually find him arched over her at the entrance to her favourite sleeping cupboard, or near the bookcase in the spare room. She managed to contort her legs and torso into an impressive upside-down thrashing rotor blade position that prevented him from being able to do her actual physical harm, but she was clearly terrified – so much so that on one occasion when I separated them, I found a small turd in the place where she'd been cowering.

Although I shied away from facing up to the reality, it was becoming obvious that there was only one course of action, and it was getting harder to convince myself that Roscoe and George 'just needed time'. Gemma kindly suggested that perhaps we might be able to find Roscoe another home, but in my mind that could never be an option: it had to be a case of first come, first served. Roscoe was the priority. Also, she was the one cat of the five who could be deemed to be more Gemma's than mine. Neither of us, especially Gemma, wanted to lose her.

There was also Ralph and Shipley to think about. More and more I was noticing how they hung back, a little unhappily, while George was around. Every day he looked stronger and healthier and seemed to improve visibly at the art of being a cat. For us, this was heart-warming and magical to watch, but for them it must have been sickening. Shipley's swearing sessions started to sound less like anti-establishment war cries and more like surly, muttered asides. It had been weeks since Ralph had hurled himself at my lap, padded me and sneezed in my face, and recently the Ralarm had been conspicuously unplugged. As I doled out affection, trying to reassure them that, despite George's easy ways, they were still more important than him, I was reminded of a conviction I'd first had a decade or so before: four cats was a lot of cats to have but it was also a safe, sane limit … for me, at least. If you were a working person, once you went over that limit an imbalance was often created, for you, but, more crucially, for the cats themselves.

I continued to kid myself that there was a solution. Roscoe had always been so fearless in the past. Why was she scared of this sunny idiot who, in every other way, seemed to be an outright pacifist? Perhaps if we shut them in a room together, she could get to know the real him and find she'd been scared of nothing all along. To my knowledge, George had never actually hurt Roscoe, but their relationship mirrored relationships between bullies and victims the world over: the more fear the victim showed, the more it egged the bully on. In the past, I'd seen the same dynamic, in much less serious form, between Shipley and The Bear. Had The Bear just stood up to him near the beginning, got right up in his face and called him a cockwomble, it probably would have defused the situation and broken the pattern, but it was never going to happen.

If my neglect to take action caused George to chase Roscoe down onto the lane and one or both of them were hit by a car, I knew I would not be able to live with myself. One wild, stormy night in late September, when they were both out of the house and I lay awake in bed worrying about this, I heard an almighty crack of thunder: the loudest I'd ever heard. It sounded as if all the thunder I'd previously witnessed had just been sensitive, acoustic thunder, and that now thunder had plugged in for the first time and formed its own rock band.

'I hate to think of her out in that,' said Gemma, who'd been woken by it.

I wandered outside and whistled a few times, but all I heard in response was the sound of branches thrashing to and fro and a small gothic owl hoot, thinned and compressed by a tunnel of wind. The only cat in evidence was The Bear, staring back at me from his perch by the pond with bright, shocked, satellite eyes.

The following morning I walked out into the dripping countryside to look for Roscoe, and discovered that the deafening crack we'd heard wasn't thunder at all but a towering red oak, a hundred yards from the house, being ripped from its roots. It lay on its side like a stunned, formerly complacent giant. A cat – particularly one as nimble as Roscoe – would surely have been able to get out of its way, but trudging through the wet grass I saw our craggy, windblown hillside through the eyes of a cat who no longer had a comfortable, relaxing home to go to, and it appeared more perilous.

When I opened the back door, the landline was ringing. This probably meant that the person on the other end was either one of my parents or one of the telesales people who often called asking for a 'Mr M', an occurrence that had, over the months, painted an image in my head of the house's former tenant as an unusually gullible secret agent.

It was my mum.

The first thing I usually say to my mum when I pick up the phone to her is, 'Hi. How are you?' But this time for some reason, perhaps her tone of voice, I said, 'Hi. Are you OK?'

It's easy to get a bit cynical about questions like 'Are you OK?', 'Are you all right?', 'How are you?' or 'How are you doing?' People often ask them knowing they won't get an authentic answer, and don't really want one, which seems to render them meaningless. But when you think a bit more deeply about these questions, they're actually a really nice part of being human. Ultimately, asking somebody how they are, even if you're not look-ing for an entirely truthful and detailed answer, is much nicer than not asking, and the impulse that makes people give a not entirely truthful and detailed answer is typic-ally a kind one: a wish not to waste someone else's time with what you perceive as your own minor troubles. And, despite what we might think, asking someone if they're OK does perform a function. It's a bigger, more sig-nificant kind of well-being check. What it often means, though we don't admit it, is, 'Is everything generally OK, and you are not desperately sad or in trouble?' especially when we put the question to somebody we truly care about. I thought about this a lot in the hours after the phone call with my mum, because, in the shaky, short silence between me asking, 'Are you OK?' and her answer, I knew what she was going to say; knew it per-haps, even, from the tone of her 'Hello' when I'd first picked up the phone.

'No, I'm really not,' she said. 'Floyd is dead.'

# Rorschach

Your inkblot prompts different reactions
It's all in the eye, and the mind, of the beholder
Some people see an alert pony's head, with a fancy ruff
Other people see a butterfly, surrounded by smaller
    relatives
Some people just see a load of ink
But everyone sees a cat
And a fine, confident one, at that
The blot somehow makes your face even more
    determined, more confident,
than it is
Which is very determined and confident indeed
You are not big yet you have never truly feared anything
Apart from maybe the computer printer
Which everyone who watched knows you totally beat
    in a fight that time
You have a friend, of your kind, of a similar colour
    scheme
But your true soulmate has two legs

A whirlwhind, like you
A carnivore, like you
A deep, unfussy rester, like you
You sleep in the same compost
And the same chair
But you always have priority in the latter location
You both seem wild, at times
But in the end, you are the only wild one
The true mystery
The one who will not be contained by the small free
    hotels of your species
Or boundary fences
Who will square off with those twice your size
And the occasional massive sheep
Was your confidence your downfall?
Maybe
But, if so, can it really be lamented?
In a life so rich and full

# YOLNT

The accident had happened on the main road, a mile from my mum and dad's house: a road that, even on my mum's most worried nights, calling Floyd's name into the silent air, she had never imagined he ventured as far as. My dad had been driving back from the swimming pool. He would have been having his usual fun there: hiding his friend Malcolm's shoes for a laugh in the changing room, and exchanging stories with the other regular swimmers, such as Danny, who'd once climbed up a ladder and mimed an obscene act with a billboard advert of Kylie Minogue. As he began to signal for the turning into the village, my dad spotted a lump of white and black fur in the road and, instantly, he'd known. 'But are you sure?' my mum had asked him when he'd arrived home and told her. 'Are you sure you saw enough to be sure?' Then, when he'd assured her, and she'd asked him again, and he'd reassured her again, he'd collected a fluorescent jacket and driven back to pick up Floyd's body – a perilous task in itself, on a single-carriageway road that dickwitted trainee Jeremy Clarksons routinely drove along at 90 mph, where an average of one fatality per year had been recorded in the decade and a half my parents had lived near it. I could picture precisely how solid and calm my dad would have been during all this. He could sometimes turn a non-crisis into a crisis, but the positive flipside of that was that when it came to an actual crisis, he was a rock.

I experienced a new emotion in the weeks that followed. I had been an adult long enough to be aware of my parents' vulnerability, to join with them in their own sadnesses and disappointments, but now something different happened: I ached on their behalf. Ached in a way that, every time I spoke to them on the phone, created a painful hollow an inch or two below my breastbone. I'd loved Floyd; over the last couple of years, his ebullient presence had made me look forward to my visits to Nottinghamshire in a whole new way. But my own feelings about him were comprehensively drowned by sympathy for what my parents were going through. After the death of their previous cat, Daisy, they'd gone five catless years – an extremely 'un-them' period. They made their excuses: they were enjoying living in a cleaner house; they wanted to be able to go on holiday without the worry of what to do with a pet while they were away. But I knew that their hesitation about plunging back into cat ownership was ultimately down to another reason that made a lot of people hesitate about adopting a pet: the knowledge of the fragility of an animal's life, and the heartbreak you open yourself up to when you make yourself responsible for that life. When they had finally caved in, they'd embraced cat ownership like never before, partly because, as a retiree and a home-worker, they had the time to do so in a way they hadn't in the past as two full-time schoolteachers, but also per-haps partly because in that catless period, a reserve of love had built up which could not help but burst forth and overflow. And also, finally, because Floyd was an easy cat to love: a small but excitable presence whose energy had become part of them. The cliché that his death had left a big gap in their house applied, but it was more than that. Their house now *was* the gap.

Of course, in the days after Floyd's accident I cuddled my cats harder than ever. 'OK, what have you done?' their eyes said. 'And should we be worried?' I was now into my fourteenth year of living with Ralph, Shipley and The Bear. I had been immensely lucky that each of them was a strong, healthy cat, and lucky too, perhaps, that they lacked (or, in The Bear's case, had long ago grown out of) the kind of wild wandering streak that Floyd had possessed. I'd lived alongside each of them for so long, their habits seemed almost an extension of my own. Here was me, going to the fridge to get a cold pick-led onion to eat, and here was Shipley, going to the fridge to climb up my leg in case I happened to get him a small chunk of turkey from a packet on the same shelf as the pickled onions. Here was me, putting on a BBC4 nature documentary and here was The Bear, sitting six inches away from my face, staring at me in a haunting, accusatory way as I watched footage of foxes mating. Here was me, going into the living room and putting on a record, and here was Ralph, following me into the living room, jumping on the sleeve of the record and knocking it onto the floor. They were all familiar actions that took place in my immediate periphery, and innate parts of what I was as a quotidian domestic being.

But this scenario wasn't going to be familiar for ever. Each of these three cats could now officially be classified as 'old' in cat years, and, in The Bear's case, more or less geriatric. If I hadn't already realised it, I would now, due to the ever-increasing number of strangers who reminded me of it on The Bear's densely populated Facebook page; nomads of the Internet who, though they'd never read my books about him, felt it their duty to stop by and inform me of his imminent demise. 'Your cat is very old now,' they told me in thoughtfully composed messages from Perth and Wrexham and and Sioux City, Iowa. 'I hope you know that it will soon be time, and you've prepared yourself.' Perhaps they took me for a not very bright person who was under the misapprehension that cats live as long as humans. I was very aware of The Bear's mortality, which was why I tried to fend it off every day by feeding him extra treats, repeatedly reminding him that I loved him and stroking him in that particular part of his chest that made him do an ecstatic tweet-purr. But the prospect of losing a cat who had lived a remarkably long, happy life could not be compared with the concept of losing a cat who was at life's zestful beginning.

Floyd's death seemed to trigger a period of unhappy events in the immediate area surrounding my mum and dad's house. Less than a day after they'd buried him, their next-door neighbour Edna, a good friend of theirs who had been a botanically inclined maternal figure to my mum since the death of my plant-loving nan five years earlier, died of a heart attack. Only four days after that, their nonagenarian neighbour on the other side, Bea, finally succumbed after a long illness. An eerie silence accompanied my mum and dad's forays into the garden.

'How are you?' I asked my dad. 'I'm OK,' he replied. 'Just sad. It hurts, but I know he had the best life possible.' I needed less than a hand's worth of fingers to count the amount of times in my life I'd heard him speak so softly.

'I keep remembering the way he'd jump on me when I was asleep in the garden, or pinch my office chair when I nipped out of the room.'

At night, my mum dreamt about little else but Floyd: sometimes the dreams were so real she would wake up feeling sure he'd walked in and been on the bed, the memory of his rain-wet fur palpable on her hands.

I wanted to drive to Nottinghamshire and whisk the two of them back here to Devon – if not for good, then at least for a fortnight, to ease their minds, to rid them at least temporarily of the constant reminders they were living with. He had been such a part of their life – sneaking into their car, sleeping in their waste-paper baskets, climbing ladders with my dad while he cleaned the windows – that every part of their house creaked eerily with his non-presence. Then on top of that, there was the difficult job of shutting out the brutality of his demise. You didn't want to think about it, but a glitch in your brain steered you back to it, told you that recognising it was something you needed to do, out of respect for him.

So much of human happiness was about this, wasn't it? How much you chose to shut out. How much of the blood-shed and war and cruelty out there in the world you let in through the portholes of your mind. How much you patted yourself on the back for saving a spider from drowning in the bath, while being unaware of the other three you potentially trod on earlier outside. How much you admit-ted to yourself the reality of all the deeply adored pet cats around the country who had been run over today, this month, this year. Shutting stuff out can be a bad habit, a selfish habit, an apathetic habit, but at times it's how we survive, especially in our new world, where every atrocity is there to see at the click of a mouse. I shut stuff out every day. If I didn't, I'd probably spend my life like The Bear, walking around, looking deep and aghast into the eyes of everyone I met, communicating in ghostly meeoops.

In the end, all you can do is carry on, clinging to that repeated, redemptive cliché of adult life: stuff almost always does get better. The key is time. Largely, as I got older, what I desired most in life was time – big chunks of it in which to write, to read, to walk, to feel free – but now I desired it in a different way; I just wanted a big chunk of it to pass, quickly, to take my parents to a point where they'd healed.

My mum, my dad, Gemma and me, all perhaps knew that there was a logical next step, cat-wise, but I wasn't going to mention it first, and I thought it best that it didn't happen until that time had passed.

In the event, it was my mum who brought it up. 'We should probably take George now, shouldn't we?' she said. 'It would make sense.'

I hemmed and hawed and made attempts to stall her, giving my reasons – my own attachment to George, and my hope that it might still work out between him and Roscoe – but, while there was a fragment of truth to these, I had an ulterior motive: I wanted to wait until my parents had grieved a little longer and were ready. I remembered from my childhood what it was like to lose a young cat suddenly in tragic circumstances and replace him rashly with another. It was not necessarily a bad thing – you were, in the end, filling an empty space with an animal's life that you hoped to quickly make better – but it could stir up a small, confusing emotional dust storm and cause a brief, acrid taste of disloyalty.

My first Devon summer had come to an end, an idyllic summer I'd spent most of somehow feeling healthier than ever and fairly seriously ill at the same time; simultaneously ecstatic at being free to be outdoors in such an amazing place, and chained to the neuroses and needs of a handful of animals which, in the loosest sense, I owned and a few others I didn't. Now autumn was coming in with a capricious vengeance uniquely characteristic of the area's microclimate. In driving evening rain its leaves advanced on the house, their damp, recently deceased faces pressed against the windows like a leaf version of *Night of the Living Dead*. I was standing in the kitchen during one

especially stormy dusk in October when I saw Shipley fly
past the window backwards. I might have worried more,
but this sort of thing happened to Shipley quite a lot. He
was wiry and immovable in some ways – especially if the
promise of turkey was in the air – but with age he'd

become prone to be whipped around in a strong breeze. In this way he was very different to his tabby brother, who could probably sit in one of his favoured 'cat monorail' poses in a strong hurricane and not even wobble.

I popped outside to check Shipley was OK. He looked a little dishevelled but appeared unharmed by his flight, and swear-meowed to confirm this fact. He should have considered himself lucky. Once you get past summer, the wind in Norfolk tends to have a vicious bite to it. In Devon the wind often pulls scarier faces, but it's got false teeth. This was a hotter place than I'd ever lived in, but I could feel something bright and warm and magical being inched away from me, like a cake on a tablecloth slowly pulled by a mystery hand. On the plus side, we had re-entered the six months of the year when the whole

county – including a large proportion of its inhabitants – smelt pleasantly of woodsmoke. In the big copse behind the house, and on my walks with Billy, I foraged eagerly for loose kindling, separating it into three grades and then pocketing it.

'You know what you've become? You've become the bloke who has cat hair on his coat and a load of kindling sticking out of his pocket,' said my friend Louise, as I came down the garden path towards her with cat hair on my coat and a load of kindling sticking out of my pocket.

Up in Nottinghamshire, my dad had an enviable relationship with the local farmer, which permitted him and his friend Philip to keep any firewood they found on the farmer's land provided they chopped it up themselves. 'PHILIP DOES THE CHAINSAWING,' he told me. 'I'M THE BRANCH MANAGER.'

This arrangement had led to a surprising number of adventures and feats of rural heroism. One of these involved my dad and Philip helping two young lovers narrowly escape from a herd of cows my dad estimated to be 'BETWEEN EIGHTY AND A HUNDRED STRONG'. In a dramatic scene straight out of a James Herriot book, the young man had tripped over at the last minute, with the cows bearing down on him, only to be hoisted over the fence by Philip in the nick of time. More dramatic still had been an incident that my dad described to me on the phone.

'I JUST FELL IN THE RIVER,' he announced. 'I FOUND THIS REALLY BRILLIANT LOG FOR FIRE-WOOD AND TRIED TO TOSS IT ACROSS THE

RIVER LIKE A CABER BUT I SLIPPED AND IT
DROPPED IN THE WATER AND THE FOOKIN' CUR-
RENT STARTED TAKING IT. BUT I RAN DOWN
THE SIDE OF THE RIVER AFTER IT REALLY FAST
AND CAUGHT IT UP ABOUT A HUNDRED YARDS
AWAY AND MADE A GRAB FOR IT BUT THEN THE
MUD SUCKED MY WELLIES OFF MY FEET.'

'Oh no!' I said. 'Then what happened?'

'THEN I FELL IN AND GOT MUD AND RIVER
WATER ALL OVER MY BEST SOCKS AND NEW
GLASSES. I GOT THE FOOKIN' LOG, THOUGH,
AND BROUGHT IT BACK. THAT'S THE MAIN
THING.'

I was glad to hear my dad sounding chirpier and louder
than he had recently. Along with going to Derbyshire
with my mum and retracing some of the walks we'd done
there as a family in the 1970s and 1980s, chopping logs
had been one of the activities that had best helped take
his mind off Floyd. It had always been one of his favourite
hobbies. Traditionally, if I arrived at my parents' house
and didn't immediately see my dad in the driveway with
his shirt off, chopping wood, it meant one of three things:
he was taking a nap, one of the weathermen he liked to
shout at was on TV at the time or dusk had fallen more
than an hour before.

All of my male relatives within living memory on my
dad's side of the family have possessed very loud voices and
been enthusiastic about firewood. I represent a slight dilu-
tion of the bloodline, in that I am enthusiastic about
firewood but only possess a voice of moderate volume.

One of my dad's loud cousin Flob's first memories of my grandad was of him and my great-grandad carrying a giant, two-man saw along their street in Nottingham, shouting excitedly, having heard a rumour that an oak had come down at a nearby farm belonging to a man called Tommy Thompson. Later, my grandad would lead my dad and Flob and the other kids in their neighbourhood on expeditions to retrieve logs from the nearby woods. My dad and Flob's teenage gang spent the coldest British month of the twentieth century, January 1963, using their spoils to make fires on the frozen canal up the road.

You can run from this kind of genetic destiny but you can only hide for so long. A decade ago in Norfolk, I'd had the Upside Down House's chimney removed: a structurally necessary, refurbishment-related decision, but one that now seems an absurd denial of what I inescapably am as a human. As I moved further into my thirties, I began to take more and more pride in my own garden bonfires, go on detours on walks solely to sniff those belonging to others, and to look at the process of felling trees in my garden almost as a form of meditation. I'd finally arrived at my current state as one of those bearded men you frequently come across in the West Country who smell of woodsmoke and start conversations about lichen in their local pub. Recently I'd even completed a forestry skills course, and proudly displayed my certificate from it on my office wall. I had cats, too, and all cats deserved a log fire, if you could possibly provide one for them. I was especially looking forward to Ralph and The Bear's resurgence as fire cats, sprawling out in front of the flames as they had done here back in early spring.

'I'VE GOT TWO THINGS TO SAY,' my dad told me. 'FIRST THING: I'M GLAD YOU GOT YOUR HAIR CUT. YOU LOOKED SHIFTY BEFORE. I CAN ALMOST TAKE YOU SERIOUSLY NOW. SECOND THING: YOU'RE GOING TO FREEZE YOUR FOOKIN' KNACKERS OFF THIS WINTER IF YOU DON'T HAVE SOME OF MY LOGS.'

He had a point: Devon might have had big-talking, toothless winds, but winter was on its way and our cottage was high on an exposed hillside; the logs I'd bought in bulk back in March had almost run out, and the ones sold by the nearest petrol station burned so poorly I'd have done no worse trying to find a sustainable heat source from a dozen Eccles cakes. But I knew that my dad was proprietorial about his firewood and I sensed, rightly, that there would be a catch.

'IT WILL WORK LIKE THIS,' he said. 'I'LL GIVE YOU A FOOKLOAD OF LOGS AND YOU GIVE US YOUR CAT IN EXCHANGE.'

I'd done some swaps in the past that might have been viewed as lopsided: a 1960s dining table for three albums by the agrarian folk musician Dick Gaughan; a Panini football sticker featuring the face of the explosive and stylish Aston Villa winger Mark Walters for one featuring that of the unexciting Chelsea midfielder Nigel Spackman. But this was the first time I'd been asked to exchange a cherished living pet for a few bags crammed full of dead tree. My parents would undoubtedly be getting the better deal here. In a couple of months' time, the logs would have run out, but George almost certainly would not. He'd still be there, providing another kind of warmth with his sunny disposition. I already envied their place in his company.

The timing was good in an additional way: 'I think we've got mice living under the sofa,' my mum had told me recently. 'They've stolen the chocolate your dad likes to keep under there.'

As I took my final few Devonian evening walks with George along the stream behind the cottage, I was struck again by what a unique bond the two of us had. In a way, we'd spent 2014 going in opposite directions – me rewilding, him dewilding – but we found ourselves in a similar place. He got on well enough with Gemma, but it felt like he knew I'd been the one responsible for turning his life around. He wanted to be with me all the time: not in a nagging or a dominant way, or even a particularly food-themed way, just in a calm way. Forsaking our life together was something he might never forgive me for, but what else could I do? Keeping him here would have been a hugely selfish gesture on my part. It would not have been fair to Roscoe, to Gemma, to my parents or to Ralph and Shipley.

A giant full moon hung over the house on the evening my parents arrived to collect him, the kind of moon that lights up the bedroom at night and makes you think it's dawn when it's really 2 a.m. Devon had these big moons a lot – somehow bolder and less neurotic than the moons you found hanging about in other parts of the country – but this was probably the biggest I'd seen since the day we moved in. I thought back to that night, and the shape that darted across the lane behind me, and there seemed

something poetic about the way these two moons book-
ended George's stay with us. The second moon's light
played on the coppery leaves behind the house and twin-
kled on the stream: George's kingdom. This terrain, this
whole region of the country, was so inimitably George, I
could barely imagine it without him. I reminded myself
that he was a cat, and no great connoisseur of rural eccen-
tricity; any nice bit of countryside was the same to him. It
wasn't as if he was going to get to the fields around my
mum and dad's house in Nottinghamshire and say, 'It's
just not the same without a woman in a smock playing a
flute in the meadow behind your garden and a man walking an owl nearby.'

Or was he?

My dad had not been joking about the logs. Pile upon pile
of them filled my parents' hatchback. When I thought he
and I had finally brought them all in and stacked them in
the porch, he arrived up the path with a large cat carrier.
This, too, was full of logs.

'RIGHT,' he said, flopping down on the sofa. 'CAN
YOU PUT ROLLING NEWS ON THE TELLY FOR ME?
I'VE BEEN UP SINCE FIVE AND WE'VE BEEN TO
THE BEACH. I'VE GOT THAT BOOK I BORROWED
OFF YOU IN MY BAG. THE ONE ABOUT THE
BLOKE WITH THE BIT IN IT WITH THE GOOSE. IS
THAT YOURS? WELL, ANYWAY, EVEN IF IT'S NOT,
IT'S GOT CHOCOLATE ON IT NOW. WHAT WE'LL

DO IS GET UP REALLY EARLY TOMORROW THEN WE'LL GET THE CAT AND GO.'

'Calm down, Mick,' said my mum. 'We've only just got here. And there are some gardens and an exhibition I'd thought I'd quite like to go and look at tomorrow.'

'I'M JUST BEING ORGANISED,' said my dad. 'SOMEONE HAS TO BE ORGANISED. WITHOUT MY ORGANISATION AND ALACRITY THIS FAMILY WOULD FALL TO BITS. AND WE CAN'T LEAVE TOO LATE BECAUSE OF THE TRAFFIC. IT'S A THURSDAY, SO THE FOOKWITS AND LOONIES WILL ALL BE OUT.'

'Why will they be out on a Thursday, in particular?' I asked.

'THURSDAY IS THE NEW FRIDAY. HAVEN'T YOU HEARD?'

I looked at George, upside down on the sofa, paws splayed, and wondered if he was ready for the tornado he was about to go and live inside. Of course, he'd spent a few days at my mum and dad's house before, but he probably just remembered that as a brief, somewhat traumatic holiday. Encountering my dad's loud jazz music and equally loud, lengthy anecdotes about his cousin Flob and tirades about Jeremy Clarkson and Alan Titchmarsh on a full-time basis was another matter entirely. I could only be thankful that he was a relatively unflappable cat, not known to be fazed by Miles Davis's more experimental late 1960s period or sudden, vociferous non sequiturs about celebrities.

'HAVE YOU STILL GOT THOSE WEIRD SEX LADYBIRDS?' asked my dad.

'Yep, they're still here,' I said.

That month, our local Devon newspaper had reported that a swarm of harlequin ladybirds had landed in Plymouth from America, a sort of seedier, reverse ladybird version of the maiden voyage of the Pilgrim Fathers on the *Mayflower* in 1609. On top of the fact that these harlequins were already responsible for ruining the clean washing of many of the city's suburban households, it was also thought that a lot of them carried Laboulbeniales fungal disease, a known STD. I couldn't be sure if the gangs of ladybirds currently congregating twenty miles east of Plymouth, on our living room door frame and bathroom window ledge, were the same ladybirds, but I was giving them a wide berth.

'I CAN'T STAND THAT GEORGE CLOONEY,' my

dad went on, gesturing at the TV, which showed George Clooney standing outside an awards ceremony, smiling at his fans and the media.

Clooney's smile was not unlike that of the other George in the room: infectious, beatific. 'What did he ever do to you?' I asked my dad.

'HE'S IN LOVE WITH HIMSELF,' he said. 'HE'S WHAT WE USED TO CALL A BIGHEAD IN THE OLD DAYS. NOBODY USES THE WORD "BIGHEAD" NOWADAYS BECAUSE IT'S OK TO BE ONE.'

'But he's George Clooney. I think really ... Shipley! Stop that!'

As we talked, Shipley, in the far corner of the room, had been attacking the waste-paper basket with a level of determination that made his morning bin-kicking sessions look casual. Now the bin tipped over and its contents spilled onto the living room floor.

'OH, I KNOW WHY HE'S DOING THAT,' said my dad. 'I PUT A DEAD CRAB IN THERE EARLIER THAT I FOUND ON THE BEACH. I THOUGHT ABOUT KEEPING IT, BUT IT WASN'T A VERY GOOD ONE.'

As all this took place, The Bear watched from his new favourite vantage point: the final slot in the wooden unit where I kept my LPs. I knew how much he liked it in there, so I'd packed the albums in the other slots very tightly in order to keep it free for him, but there were some very good second-hand record shops in Devon and soon the inevitable overspill would take place, with the likes of Stevie Wonder, Neil Young and ZZ Top forcing

The Bear out. No doubt he'd find another surveillance point soon enough, from where he could watch the absurd affairs of humans and mortal cats and make notes on them to take back eventually to his superior home planet. He'd become a little more zen and unflappable in the eight months since we'd moved here. There was a time when, with Shipley on one of his vandalistic rampages, The Bear would have quickly made himself scarce, but he seemed less fazed by them these days, or by Shipley in general.

I put this down partly to The Bear's failing hearing. Living with Shipley – especially around mealtimes – was a lot like living with a large furry meatfly: much of the intimidation factor came from a constant, aggressive buzzing sound combined with insistent, restless movement. Once you took the noise away, there was a lot less to fear. When Shipley strutted in The Bear's direction, The Bear now no longer heard his approach, so no longer shrank from it, and with this some of the joy seemed to go out of the chase for Shipley. The Bear would often not even realise he was being harassed until Shipley's face appeared over his shoulder. 'Oh! It's you!' The Bear seemed to say at these points: a little shocked, but without fear. A couple of minutes later, the two of them would be found sitting quite peacefully together, the poet and the fool of my medieval cat court, finally harmonious after years of rancour. It was a good lesson on the psychology of bullying; Shipley's persistent, aggressive balloon had been popped solely by The Bear's transcendental calm. That said, The Bear was still very protective about his Bearhole in the garden, and would issue a warning gargle if Shipley tried to join him in it.

I liked to think that The Bear's growing serenity was also down to the time he'd spent with George recently. I'd found George backwards-spooning him again, and The Bear certainly didn't look unhappy about it. Would he miss his idiot pal? Perhaps not. The following morning there were no choked-up goodbyes from The Bear as George's carrier was brought into the living room. I was another matter entirely. It was my job to load George into his plastic travel prison because Gemma was at work by then and, well, ultimately, how could it be anyone else's? I reminded myself that it could be worse: he could be going to live with a stranger, and I might never see him again. At least I had visitation rights. Who knows? Maybe one day he might even move back to Devon. But there was something very final about the moment when I locked the clasp on his carrier, something that made me realise I had never been fully committed to our previous goodbye. The simple, sad look on his face as he stared back at me through the bars, betrayed and uncompre-hending, would stay with me for weeks.

About a month after George left, I took The Bear to see the vet. The lump on his back had returned, slightly bigger than before, and this time it didn't mysteriously vanish when the vet examined it. The vet said it was a cyst, but nothing to worry about or that would require an operation. I wish I could have said the same for my own lump. Going to my own special human vet to have it removed had become such a regular occurrence for me that I'd started to view it as a little like having a haircut; the only real dif-ference being that it happened more frequently and

nobody asked me if I was going anywhere nice for my holidays this year. If my doctor *had* asked me if I'd been going anywhere nice for my holidays this year, I would have told him the truth, which was that I didn't have proper holidays, due to the fact that I lived with four demanding cats. Three of them were getting on a bit now, but this most ancient of them was doing pretty well, to say the least. He'd lost a tiny bit of weight recently and his appetite had increased significantly, and the vet confirmed my suspicion that The Bear was suffering from a slightly overactive thyroid. This was normal for a cat in his twentieth year, and the vet and I agreed that, in view of his age and the level of the problem, it was best just to monitor it for now, rather than put The Bear through the stress of any of the treatments available.

I remembered four years ago when another of my cats, Janet, who'd been suffering from a much more extreme case of hyperthyroidism, had died very suddenly. In the aftermath of that, The Bear, the older of the two cats, had seemed to be the unlikely survivor. Since then people, whether strangers or friends, had warned me so often about his imminent demise. And now here he was, much older, the survivor again, with poorer hearing and less easily retractable claws, but other than that largely, astoundingly, the same: a cat who was precisely the age of the second Oasis album but to whom time had been far kinder. If I was honest with myself, a year ago, in that dark bungalow, sur‑rounded by diesel fumes and the clang of skips, with Gymcat lurking outside, I could not have pictured The Bear here now, in this good place. In fact, it would have been quite a stretch to picture myself here, too. His hearing was definitely going, but it didn't seem to be troubling him. If anything, the opposite was true: the main effects, as well as diminishing Shipley's presence, were that he seemed amazingly pleased to see me or Gemma when we miracu‑lously and soundlessly appeared beside him in the garden, and that his new friendly bee sound and sessions of meoop‑ing at his favourite water bowl became louder and more ebullient than ever. Sometimes, the love that he felt for his water bowl was so deep he'd curl up and sleep beside it on the bathroom floor. His affection for it was understand‑able. Devon, particularly the region around Dartmoor, does have some of the UK's best water.

As winter came in hard, I fed The Bear more treats than ever: high‑end tunas, chicken drumsticks, prawns. It

was my way of keeping him happy, going by the philo-
sophy that happiness creates longevity, but it was also my
attempt to find ways to thank him. Over the last few
years, I had come to view him as a lucky charm as well as
a friend, a sort of watchful, furry warden of my life.

In less of a show of gratitude, I had finally filled the
empty slot on the unit where I kept my LPs, edging The

Bear out. At night, he and Ralph now curled up a few feet to the right of it next to the fire and, when I went to bed, I put an extra log on for them – partly out of kindness, but also because time has taught me that cats remember everything. Both of them had turned into ardent fire cats, a habit that pleased me immensely. Shipley, meanwhile, remained nervous around the hearth, and Roscoe preferred the softer warmth of a human midriff. At night, she burrowed fiercely into any available person. It took her a while to come fully back to us, and, weeks after George's departure, she still looked anxiously over her shoulder every time she arrived in the kitchen doorway or by the sofa in the living room, George's favoured ambush spots. From her point of view she probably could not believe he was gone because, by all cat logic, she could see no good reason why he would be gone. He wouldn't just decide to leave, after all. He had it too good here. But by tiny increments, she withdrew her guard and let herself believe. Outdoors, she became confident more quickly, and transmogrified into the old Roscoe, smacking Shipley into line with one paw and getting on with hedgerow admin with another. She was a Diana Rigg of cats: dainty but menacing, although with a bit less of the dainty now that winter weight of hers was piling back on. As she followed me up through the skeletal, lichen-furred trees behind the garden to the waterlogged meadow, stripped of its flowers, I realised something about her battle with George: a big part of it might in fact have been territorial all along. The cat who owned this land was gone. Now she had moved in, unchallenged, and annexed the whole lot.

I'd been convinced that, once George had gone, another interloper would soon follow, but there'd been nothing. Two days after he'd left I'd noticed a flash of grey behind the garden fence and thought it was the return of Fluffy Grey Poo Burglar Cat, but it had just been a squirrel. Almost as far back as I could remember there had been an outsider cat – usually homeless, sometimes just downright obnoxious – trying to muscle in on my cats' party, but now a rare period free of invasion began, and its effects showed. Each of them became bigger versions of themselves. I realised, really realised, for the first time how truly subdued Ralph and Shipley had been during George's tenure here. Mostly, Gemma and I were happy to have them 100 per cent back with us, but there were times – those, for example, when Shipley stole some toast or clawed his way swearing up the back of the chair I was sitting on, or when Ralph walked about the house at 4 a.m.

pulling stuff off shelves, meowing his own name and sitting in plant pots – when we felt more conflicted about it.

My mum had always felt that my attempt to make George part of our household was a mistake, but she knew what a wrench it was for me to let go of him and her updates about his new life in Nottinghamshire came thick and fast. The one early bump in his progress was Bonfire Night, during which he hid under their spare bed. This was in sharp contrast to Shipley, who, at the first sign of fireworks had walked outside, more or less held his paws out wide to the night air and defiantly announced, 'Bring it.' Fireworks, it transpired, were George's one other fear besides the cupboard under the stairs in his old home. My dad's booming voice and 1960s African pop albums and loud footsteps, Sooty the local delinquent cat from three doors away, the thug hedgehogs who'd attacked my mum's slippers, the cows in the

field behind the garden – none of these things held any trepidation for him. As for Casper, their friendship took no time at all to develop and, while not without its rough and tumble aspect, left Casper slightly less dishevelled than his relationship with George's predecessor.

'George and Casper talk to each other a lot,' my mum told me. 'They do this wibbling thing at one another. Then, if they're tired, they'll sometimes go up to the bed and sleep next to one another. George has this new noise, too, kind of like a quiet cockerel.'

I felt torn, hearing this news. I was relieved George was settling in well. On the other hand, what exactly was this quiet cockerel noise, and why hadn't he made it for me? Perhaps he reserved his quiet cockerel noise solely for people he truly loved. Maybe, in fact, what the quiet cockerel noise meant was: 'I prefer you to the heartless Tom, who so coldly gave me away, after everything he and I had been through.'

My parents had both had a strong relationship with Floyd, but he'd been my dad's feline soulmate. George had no hesitation in jumping on my dad's stomach as he read at night, but his calm temperament was more of a match for my mum. He spent most of his time in my mum's work-room, at the rear of the house. The sheer amount of creativity that emerged from this room every month was staggering, more redolent of a 1960s Manhattan loft's worth of bohemians than one retired schoolteacher from Liverpool not much over five feet tall. My mum had post-poned her true vocation in life for four decades, but now that she was finally giving it a go, she wasn't wasting any time. As my mum sewed, cut, printed, etched and painted, George sat nearby. Inevitably, he became her muse. After less than a month, she had already made her own linocut of him. From the shape of this, I sensed his gastronomic life had already improved.

Unlike Floyd, George did not stray far from the house, but when he arrived back, he was usually keen to tell her of his exploits. Sometimes, though, his enthusiasm could

get the better of him, with perilous results. 'I'd just put a load of prints out to dry and I saw him arrive in the room and launch himself towards the table,' my mum told me. 'I launched myself towards him at almost exactly the same time and caught him in mid-air, like a rugby ball.'

I could picture this scene vividly, and it made me laugh, but it also made me a bit envious – partly because I wished I had the talent to make lovely linocuts of hares and foxes and cats, but also because I wanted to be able to catch George in mid-air too. I could still clearly remember the ever-softening feel of his fur; what a big, floppy lump of pliable hippie cat he was.

In the famous viral YouTube clip of Christian The Lion, Christian – a lion bought, bewilderingly, from Harrods in 1969 by John Rendall and Anthony Bourke – is seen running joyfully into the arms of his former owners a year after being released into the Kenyan wilderness. This pretty much encapsulates the way I'd pictured my first reunion with George in the days leading up to Christmas 2014. What actually happened is that he strolled lazily into my parents' kitchen, looked up at me with an insouciant 'Oh, it's you' expression, then said 'Geeeeooorge' to my mum, in the hope that she would feed him more of the expensive brand snacks he had become addicted to. George soon warmed to me, and spent a large portion of Christmas Day sitting on my lap looking stoned as my dad told stories about teacher–pupil brawls in Nottingham inner city schools in the 1970s. Later, he stared meditatively at a candle for a full half-hour, mesmerised by the flame. I was coming to the acceptance, however, that this was not my hippie cat that I'd loaned

out; this was now my mum and dad's hippie cat. On Boxing Day, the three of us watched him shin confidently up the cherry tree in their garden, entirely at home outdoors as well as indoors, in his new environment.

'What a dickhead,' I said.

'DON'T TALK ABOUT YOUR MUM LIKE THAT,' said my dad.

That night, George got a shock; a mysterious white substance he'd never seen before fell from the sky and covered
the ground. Tentatively venturing out into it the next
morning, he got an even bigger shock as a large lump of it
fell from the porch roof, covering him almost completely.
Casper, accustomed to snow, made the most of its camou-
flage possibilities, jumping out at George from behind
bushes. The two of them gambolled about in it then fell
asleep, paws touching, in front of the fire in my mum and
dad's living room. It was clear that it was George's house,
though, and Casper was, in the end, just a guest. I sensed
something a little different about George's overall manner;
something I kidded myself was hurt and a cold mourning
for the rural South West, but which was probably just a
new nonchalance at his unrivalled place at the centre of a
domestic universe. Whatever the case, he had found
something here that he had striven so hard for at my
house and not quite found: a friend of his own species.

I doubt whether any of my other cats could truly call
each other 'friends', although they accepted each other
more freely than they had in the past. With George gone,
The Bear and Roscoe rekindled their alliance somewhat,
with Roscoe occasionally to be found asleep spreadeagled
across The Bear's back. One day, a cat food company sent
me a taster package, and the courier from the firm they'd
employed to deliver it arrived at the front door looking flustered. Apparently, the company had decided to address the
package to two of my cats, rather than to me. 'I've been
driving around for an hour looking for a pub called The
Bear and Roscoe,' the courier told me. It would probably

have been a good pub, and Roscoe had a fair amount of experience in that area, but the name put me more in mind of an American cop show about two reluctant buddies: the old renegade, who keeps promising to retire, and the fastidious youngster, obsessed with paperwork and doing everything by the book. Such a partnership could never happen in real life, though. Roscoe was far too busy. She now prowled the countryside around the house, unchallenged: an outdoorsy country cat who, like me, probably could barely even remember that brief period of being a big city cat. We saw her at night, as she tunnelled stubbornly into us for warmth, and she would often deign to greet us with a high five or two on the garden path when we arrived home, but other than that she was mostly away on business.

I took The Bear to the vet again early in the new year and learned that his lump, his weight and his thyroid condition had not deteriorated. His unretracted claws made

him sound like a miniature tap dancer as he skittered across our small living room's ancient wood floor but, with a new boldness, he skipped nimbly up onto our coffee table when we weren't looking and attempted to steal chips and broccoli. Shipley frequently followed, and let out a 'Mrrreewwwwegh' noise, which I assumed was cat for 'I really hate you since you've been a vegetarian'. Was it possible that both of them actually looked healthier than they'd done in the autumn? As February – winter's inevitable, much prayed against encore – arrived, I found myself willing The Bear through it towards the day when he felt the first spring sun on his fur.

There were a couple of brief flurries of snow in our part of Devon, but none of it settled. It was different up on the highest part of Dartmoor, where I walked with my friend Mike towards winter's end. Four miles into our ramble, a bank of snow fog descended, visibility became little more than twenty yards and sleet pounded our anorak hoods at such a furious volume it was hard to hear our own voices. For Mike, an experienced mountaineer who'd spent years as an integral part of the Dartmoor rescue team, this was nothing, and he casually stopped every few yards to tell stories, as if we were walking through a water meadow beside a river on a balmy, butterfly-speckled day in July.

Our conversation somehow got on to the feral cat he'd adopted several years ago at his isolated cottage here on the moor. 'We essentially got him from Death Row,' he said. 'He was called Wallace, short for William Wallace, as in Braveheart. He was the one cat at the rescue centre that nobody wanted, and he'd been cordoned off in his own room. They didn't even do their usual home visit to check we were suitable owners. They just told us to take him.' When Mike had bought his house, he'd opened the door to the shed where the electricity generator was kept to what he called 'a fountain of rats'. He would have liked a friendly cat, but what he was fundamentally looking for was a pest-control pet. He made a bed for Wallace in one of his other outbuildings and, while Wallace virtually scratched the door down during his one foray into the house and never let anyone stroke him or pick him up, he caught hundreds of rats over the next decade until, last year, he died crossing the road near the house.

This was perhaps not a typical stray cat adoption story, but it reminded me of how lucky we'd been with George. All the homeless cats I'd known in the past had a noticeable anxiety or mental scar, however obscure, but George was different: he greeted life with balance and easy poise, as if he'd come from somewhere kind and good – but not too kind and good. Now my mum and dad were desperate to know his story, just as I had been.

'He's a mystery man,' said my mum. 'He's all ease and happiness on the surface, but I think he has a lot of secrets, deep down, which he will never tell anyone.'

'HE WON'T STOP EATING AT THE MOMENT,' added my dad. 'HE'S JUST LIKE ALL THE DOPE-SMOKING HIPPIES I USED TO KNOW IN THE SEVENTIES: ALWAYS GOBBLING BISCUITS.'

It's spring now, and I'm just back from my second visit to see my mum and dad and George in Nottinghamshire. I noticed another change in George while I was there. It wasn't just that he looked healthy and well cared for; he has now begun to look almost ... posh. He's become the kind of cat you feel a nagging need to put next to some fresh flowers and render in ink, even if you haven't got an artistic bone in your body. My mum insists he still takes care of all his own personal hygiene, but he appears impossibly clean and fragrant, almost as if freshly tumble-dried. The initial scratched-up incarnation of him I'd known is now almost unimaginable. He and Casper wrestled, in a friendly way, not long after I arrived but George seemed to have the upper hand. Later, they walked from the kitchen to the living room in perfect synchronicity, tails locked together: cats who, while not identical, find themselves on a similarly mellow spiritual plane. The weather changed for the better a couple of days after that. Overexcited, George leapt through the bathroom skylight and slid down the roof, claws screeching on the tiles, looking imploringly back at my mum. He managed to hold on and climb back in, and half an hour later he was in the garden, watching from a tree in the sunshine as my dad spread his feted 'black gold' compost on the flower beds.

I've been sitting outside in the good weather today with my somewhat more motley cats. It's that special kind of spring warmth that makes felines strut around even more like they own the world than normal. Today, you just know that cats everywhere are acting like they rule the world. Or perhaps that should be 'acting even more like they rule the world than normal.' I'm excited at the prospect of a summer in this magical, green place without being stifled by illness. I noted earlier, driving into town, that the 'Twinned with Area 51' sign has now been changed back to 'Twinned with Narnia'. There's a general feeling of change about, as if winter's old, doomy air has been sucked away and and a new, positive, spring variety has been piped in.

Shipley has just been on my lap, upside down, contracting his paws on an invisible surface above him, playing a cat version of air guitar. I didn't actually notice him appear. That's one of Shipley's special talents: he's the loudest, most boisterous cat I know, but is capable, when it suits him, of feats of extreme stealth. Ralph is rolling on a paving slab in a spot of sunlight, ecstatic to be Ralph, as ever, not looking a day over nine. Roscoe has just skipped by, feinting towards me then away, like a nimble winger in a cat football team, and is now peering into the hedgerow, her head down over some work. The Bear is here too, sunning himself near my feet: alert, eager-eyed, polite, a little plumper than he was in November. The Bear is always here, not often the biggest part of the action but close to it, ever observing. How many lives is it he's been through, now? I've lost count. My willing him through to this blossoming, perfect April day was needless. If you overlook the day about a month ago when he fell in the pond, he made it with ease. He is, after all, The Bear.

There has been no talk between Gemma and me of finding a replacement for George. These four cats are easily enough for us. As to dogs, I'm very happy to continue borrowing, rather than owning, one of those. Dogs are mostly great, but I'm not sure I respect their critical judgement quite as well as I do that of cats. If a cat recommended a record to me, I'd listen diligently. If a dog did the same, I'd probably respond in some polite but noncommittal manner then ignore its suggestion entirely. Billy and I have continued on our weekly walks, in which I lecture him on new facts I've learned about Devon history while he feigns interest and twangs about the countryside like some elastic posing as a black ball of wool. In February, on one of this winter's angriest, stormiest nights, Susie had a scare when he vanished from the house of another local friend who was looking after him. When I found her phone message at 5 a.m. I got dressed instantly and was ready to join the search party. He was found not long afterwards, but prior to that I had a sudden, potent awareness of his vulnerability, out there in the gale-force winds with little road sense; a vulnerability far more scary than Roscoe's, during her disappearance last year. This is perhaps another reason why cats remain my sole official pets – overlooking the STD-carrying ladybirds and the moths, both of which are back with a vengeance.

There have been rabbits, too, but not as many as there were this time last year, and I'm trying to blot most recent episodes involving them out of my mind. I managed to save one Ralph brought in earlier, but then I felt bad and apologised to him: yesterday, Easter Sunday, we ran out of cat food and the supermarkets were closed, meaning all he had to eat last night were biscuits, so it's only logical he should get a meal of his own, and his choice was neatly appropriate to the season. I do wish, though, that someone would come up with a microchip cat flap that would only let your cat in if he *and* the animal he was carrying in his mouth were both chipped. It's right up there near the top of the list of feline-related inventions I'd most like to see, along with food sachets that don't squirt jellified meat up your arm every time you open them.

Ralph seems to have accepted my apology now. He's just waltzed over and licked Shipley's ear, then bitten it, then enthusiastically nutted my hand and meowed his own name. What he'd like to do right now, I am aware, is get on my chest, kick my laptop to the floor, pad and dribble on me then sneeze in my face. Out of all these cats, he's the one whose affection seems to be the least related to where his next meal is coming from. His motivation is the desire for companionship, and to invite a human to join him in glorying in his magnificence. This is perhaps nothing new; it's an arrangement that's been going on between cats and the more manipulable side of humankind for several thousand years. With George gone, he has been returned to his place as Hippie King, high above – at least in his mind – the other members of his court: the fool, the poet and, over there in that bush, the elusive, diminutive but intimidating lawyer figure, who often pulls the strings.

I imagine this scene going on right now is similar to one of those George watched from some dark corner on the margins of the garden exactly a year ago. I will almost certainly never know where his life started, and it boggles my mind and troubles me to try to imagine what situation could have created a cat so lovely, yet so lonely, so I tend not to think about that part. I've frequently pictured the bit after, though – the new story that starts from the day I moved to Devon – and I see it a bit like this: He has wandered very far, and encountered lots of people and other cats along the way. There have been moments of hope, but there have been obstacles too – locked doors, dogs, roads – and he's been on the move for a long time, long enough to feel his own body grow, even in its malnourished state. As he crosses the road in front of the stone cottage under the big moon, he sees the tired man and woman get out of the car carrying what seems to be cats, in boxes. Something about this – and something a little bit soft and gullible in the man's manner that he recognises in his own – triggers his interest. Is this, finally, what he's been looking for? He waits around for almost a week and doesn't see any cats. He survives on rabbits and a few old scraps of leftover chips and burger he finds on tables outside the pub, at the time when the sandy-coloured cat who lives there isn't around.

Then one day he spots them: four of them, in total. A loud, sweary one, a big, unusually hairy one who looks inordinately happy with himself, a gentle intellectual one and a black and white, industrious-looking one who makes his hormones tingle and buzz. He decides the gentle intellectual one is his best chance of an 'in', but when he tries to befriend him, something entirely unexpected happens: the gentle intellectual one is skilled in cat martial arts, and lashes out with a series of complicated flying kicks. It's not a good start, and things get worse when, on a cold night, a big splash of water hits his head from above. He is tempted to give up, but he doesn't. There is something here, he is sure; he has sensed it. And one day, just as he is starting to feel as if maybe he is not welcome, a dish full of food appears outside the house. There is nobody else around, but he senses a human presence, watching him. Could the food be for him? Or is it a trap? He is hungry, but he's feeling wounded from having his initial bold overtures rebuffed. His instinct brought him here, though, and his instincts have been solid in the past; they are, after all, what's kept him alive until now, against some pretty tall odds.

He decides to be brave, and finds a little trust within himself and moves towards the food. Because, if you don't live with at least a little trust, what do you have left, except darkness?

# Acknowledgements

A huge thanks to my editor, Hannah Boursnell, to my agent Ed Wilson, to Rhiannon Smith, Gemma Conley-Smith, Helen Upton and everyone else at Little Brown, and to Marcia Markland, Quressa Robinson, Joanie Martinez, Joan Higgins and the team at St Martin's Press. My mum and dad deserve special mention here, for being lovely and funny, for encouraging me to read books and take an interest in the natural world from an early age and, in my dad's case, for giving this book its title (the compost, axe and chocolate are in the post). A massive thank you too to Gemma, for her support and patience, especially on that day when I left the tap on because I was thinking too hard about moths.

Twitter has been enormously helpful in the extended life of all four of my catoirs, and I wonder if this one would even exist without it, so I raise a glass to the self-named 'Bear's Army': Awkward Prawn, Anna Hales, Sarah Lery, Christina Smith, Diane Lindsay, Welsh Felix, Miranda Whiting, Ellen Zahl, Amanda Aston, StryderBourke, Jo Short, MoggsyG, Bogey, Sian Kennedy, Stacy Merrick, Sidonie Dao Vu, Jo Short, Andy Mac, PixiePippi, Jo Plumridge, Helen Thompson, Sandy F2000 and everyone else who has ever sent me a nice tweet about my work. The online encouragement of writers I've never met but whose words I admire has also been a big help. Elizabeth McCracken, Jane Fallon, Ben Myers, Sathnam Sanghera, Rob Cowen, Nancy Franklin – thank you all.

Cheers also to Chloe Hukin and her colleagues at *Your Cat* magazine, Susie Jackson for Billy, Billy for being Billy, Deborah and David for being great neighbours, my good pals Pal Bristow and Laura Manners for their eternal words of encouragement, Stephen Dray for the website, Pete Small for the owls, and the excellent county of Devon, for making this book more colourful than it probably would have otherwise been.

If you enjoyed reading about The Bear, Ralph,
Shipley and Roscoe, you can keep up-to-date
with their antics in a variety of ways:

Twitter
The Bear: @MYSADCAT
Ralph: @MYSMUGCAT
Tom: @cox_tom
Use the hashtag #goodbadfurry to talk about the
book.

Facebook
www.facebook.com/pages/Under-The-
Paw/93407930986

Pinterest
www.pinterest.com/goodbadfurry/

Blog
www.tomcoxblog.blogspot.co.uk

Tom's website
www.tom-cox.com